TECHNI

OF

HARASSMENT

TECHNIQUES
OF
HARASSMENT

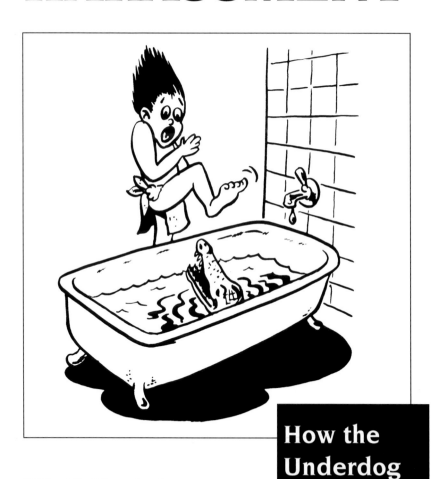

**How the
Underdog
Gets Justice**

VICTOR SANTORO

PALADIN PRESS • BOULDER, COLORADO

Techniques of Harassment: How the Underdog Gets Justice
by Victor Santoro

Copyright © 1984 by Victor Santoro
ISBN 13: 978-0-87364-298-9
Printed in the United States of America

Published by Paladin Press, a division of Paladin Enterprises, Inc.
Gunbarrel Tech Center, 7077 Winchester Circle
Boulder, Colorado 80301 USA
+1.303.443.7250

Direct inquiries and/or orders to the above address.

Cartoons by Jordan L. Cooper

Visit our Web site at www.paladin-press.com

Warning

The information in *Techniques of Harassment* is *for entertainment purposes only*. The author, publisher, and distributors assume no responsibility for the use or misuse of the contents of this book.

Table of Contents

Introduction

All of us have, at one time or another, wanted to "get" someone. For various motives, such as jealousy, revenge, the desire to right some injustice, we wish to see someone harmed or at least to be made to feel extremely uncomfortable. If we act impulsively, in a fit of anger, we may wind up in jail facing a charge of assault or even murder. Few situations justify killing someone. Fortunately most of us do not lose our tempers easily. It's a lot safer that way.

1

Often, too, the situation doesn't look the same to us the next morning, after we've cooled off and had a chance to think calmly and rationally about it. We're more inclined to "forgive and forget".

But what if we can't "forgive and forget"? What then?

First, remember that while generally it is a good thing to keep your temper you are under no moral obligation to swallow anything and everything that someone tries to shove at you. You don't have to turn the other cheek while someone keeps on slapping you.

In many cases the law will protect you. There are libel laws, cease and desist orders, small claims courts, etc. Sometimes these will work for you. Sometimes they won't. When they don't you are on your own.

Two examples will adequately illustrate the type of situation which forms the basis for discussion:

You are new on the job. Your boss accuses you of theft. You are innocent. You can prove it and you do. Your boss is not man enough to admit he was wrong and to apologize to you. He fires you instead. There is no union to stick up for you. A lawyer would be expensive and you're not sure what he could do for you. Besides you are fed up and no longer want the job.

You've just rented an apartment. You've paid a month's rent in advance and a month's security deposit. When you go to move in you see that the apartment has been left in such a filthy condition that you can't live there. The landlord refuses to clean it up and he won't give you your money back, even though you did not move in. You go to small claims court and get a summons for him. You take time off without pay from your job but the landlord does not appear for the hearing. A new date is set but he still doesn't show and you've lost more time from your job. Under pressure from the court he does appear at the third hearing but you only get your security deposit back, not the month's rent. You're also out the pay you lost during your time in court.

Both of these cases are real cases that happened to real people. If something such as this had happened to you you'd be justifiably angry. You would have been badly treated by someone why knew fully what he was doing. In both cases

2

the law was not much help. You'd want some sort of satisfaction. You would not, if you were wise, do anything extreme and illegal that could get you into worse trouble but you'd want to cause someone as much trouble as he'd caused you. What could you do?

The answer is harassment. Not anything as crude as threatening phone calls or slashing his tires. Nothing that will cause you as much trouble as it causes it him. Instead, a carefully planned and systematic program of harassment which will disrupt his life while exposing you to no risks.

Most of the techniques outlined here have been used successfully. A few have not been tried but are a logical outgrowth of ones that have been. Most are not illegal. The ones that are, like most of the techniques in here, expose you to no risk at all.

Harassment is a subject that has received little study. Most people are inclined to take direct and violent action or to do nothing at all. Harassment is the middle road, for situations that are not all that serious and yet leave you with the feeling that you must do something.

One recent use of harassment that made the front page is that employed by some members of the Committee to Re-elect the President during what has come to be known as the Watergate affair. These agents of CREEP traveled around the country stalking Democratic candidates. They phoned in to cancel their hotel reservations, ordered pizzas to be delivered to them, made up offensive bumper stickers to embarrass the Democrats at their rallies, etc. They were effective far out of proportion to their number.

3

Selecting Your Target

Whom do you hit? This is a very important question. You can't go around indiscriminately harassing anyone who rubs you the wrong way. You'd spend your entire life settling grudges and this is a pretty negative way to live. There are two questions you should ask yourself before starting on any program of harassment:

Would most of your friends feel that you had a justifiable complaint?

Is it worth the effort?

If the answer to both of these questions is yes, then you probably have good reason to begin. If, however, the answer to the first one is no, then you should think very carefully about the whole thing. There are two sides to every story and what might seem like a great injustice to you might seem to be an unfortunate misunderstanding to a third person.

Assuming you have decided to hit someone the next question is when. The timing can be very important. As a general rule, it is a good idea to let enough time go by so that he forgets about you, or forgets that you are mad at him. Don't be impatient. Remember; revenge is the only dish that tastes best when eaten cold.

Here are a few examples to help you judge the timing. If your complaining is against a landlord, you can probably act within a few weeks or months. He probably has other unhappy tenants and he knows it. If you have been fired from a job, don't act right away. It might be wise to wait a year or two. A boss always thinks first of disgruntled employees or ex-employees.

If your target is unaware that you have any conflict with him, you can act immediately. One such target would be the company spy who befriends his fellow workers and then tells the boss whatever derogatory information he has been able to discover about them. In that case it is important not to confront him. Even if what he has told the boss threatens your job don't let him know that you know. Keep up a friendly front to him and in fact exploit him to find out information which you can use in your planning.

A good general rule to follow is to give your target time enough to antagonize several other people before you act. This will increase the number of suspects when things start happening to him. If he is as unpleasant a person as you think he is you can be sure that many other people will share your feelings about him.

6

The Basic Strategies

The fundamental idea is to cause as much harassment and discomfort to your target as possible without being discovered. You can see, from studying the techniques, that if your target finds out who is harassing him he can do the same things to you. If that happens the best defense for you is to leave town. There is also the possibility of a civil suit.

There are several basic strategic principles to follow for best results:

PREPARE YOUR PLAN AS CAREFULLY AND COMPLETELY AS POSSIBLE BEFORE YOU MAKE YOUR MOVE.

Put it in writing in the form of a chart. Get a large piece of paper and lay out your planned moves in chronological order, by date. By using this basic framework to coordinate the various parts of your plan you will avoid your plans conflicting with each other.

GET ALL THE NECESSARY INFORMATION ON YOUR TARGET BEFORE YOU MAKE YOUR FIRST MOVE

You will need to know many things about your target as you develop your plan, such as his home and business addresses, phone numbers, daily schedule, the make, color, and license number of his car, etc.

AVOID ALL PERSONAL CONTACT WITH HIM WHILE CARRYING OUT YOUR PLAN

Don't come near his home or job. Don't call him at home. He might recognize your face or your voice and start putting two and two together. If you must call his home to see if he answers, do it from a public phone. If you must approach his address to find out whether he lives in a house or apartment, do it well before you start your plan moving.

USE THE MULTIPLIER EFFECT AS MUCH AS POSSIBLE

This means, in plain language, let others do the work for you. That way, you can set in motion a much greater effect on his life than if you did it all by yourself. For example, don't annoy him by constantly phoning him at all hours. You'll only tie up your time for those hours. A classified ad in a newspaper will cause other people to phone him. As you will see from the following chapters, there are many ways in which one phone call from you can tie up his time for many hours and cause him a degree of harassment entirely out of proportion to your effort.

The Need for Accurate Information

This deserves a chapter all to itself. When planning your offensive you will see that you need certain information about your target in order to carry out each phase of your plan. You should get all the information you can on your target before you make your first move. Since obtaining some of the information may expose you to some personal contact, it is essential that you do this when nothing has yet happened to make him suspicious.

The basic data you need are: name, home and business addresses, home and business phones, type of car he drives, and its color and license number. Often you can find out what you need to know about his car just by driving by his house.

Almost as important are the answers to these questions:

Does he own his own home or live in an apartment?

Is he self-employed or does he work for someone else?

What kind of work does he do?

What is his position in the company?

What hours does he work?

Does he spend most of his off-duty time at home?

Is he married? Children?

Does he travel much? Does he make out of town business trips? When? By car? Plane?

What airline? When? How often? If you know this you can have fun with his reservations.

In what hotels does he stay? You can send him telegrams there.

What are his hobbies? When does he go on vacation?

Does he own a boat? Where does he keep it?

Every bit of information you can get about him opens him up to further harassment if you have the basic know-how and the imagination to make use of it.

Let Your Fingers Do the Walking

The yellow pages of your telephone directory will be your basic source of goods and services by phone. You can impersonate your target over the phone and have a surprising variety and quantity of things delivered to his house or place of business. The basic technique is to pick up the yellow pages, start at "A" and work your way through to "Z".

One caution is necessary, however. Do not send the police or fire department to his house. This is strictly illegal and it could get an innocent person killed. Too, most police and fire departments tape their calls and you don't want your voice on tape.

Some examples from the phone book are:

Phone a liquor store late at night, shortly before it closes. Tell them you are Mr.— and that you're having a party. A radio turned up loudly in the room will make this more credible. Tell the clerk you're running out of booze and order a couple of cases. If the clerk shows any reluctance at all or seems hesitant, offer him a ten dollar tip if he can deliver within fifteen minutes to a half hour. If your target goes to bed early this will be doubly effective in disturbing him.

Look for a florist who takes telephone orders and charges them to your telephone bill. Tell him you are Mr.— and order a bouquet (an expensive one, of course) to be delivered to his wife while he is away at work. In order to ensure that the wife will accept it, order it to be inscribed on the card; "To my loving wife on a very special occasion." This will overcome awkward details such as not knowing his wife's name or birthday. Have it charged to his phone bill, of course.

If you know where he parks his car, phone an auto repair service and have it towed away.

Phone contractors, swimming pool companies, exterminators, etc. to stop by and give him estimates. You can see why it is important to know when he'll be home.

This is easier than it seems. There is no problem to impersonating your target over the phone when ordering goods and services in his name. The people you will call probably do not know your target and in any event, one voice on the phone sounds pretty much like any other.

Special Telephone Techniques

If you normally work nights and get off late, or if you're on your way home from a party late at night you can disturb his sleep by dialing his number from a phone booth and hanging up as soon as he answers. Do not ever call him from your home, as it is possible nowadays to trace a call in seconds. Do not ever say anything when calling him — you don't want to risk him taping your voice. He might have a tape recorder hooked up after a few days of this treatment.

When calling for salesmen to come out and give demonstrations or estimates, try to get them to come at unusual hours. Tell them that you work evenings and you would appreciate it if they could come after ten p.m. You can do the reverse of this too. If you know that your target sleeps normally until eight or nine in the morning you can request that the representative come at seven. If he wants to phone before coming that's fine too.

If you don't know what car your target drives call his home when he is away and tell his wife or other relative that you represent a consumer research organization and that you are conducting a survey on car owner satisfaction and frequency of repairs. Ask for the car make, year, color, and license plate number. Ask appropriate questions about the car's repair history in order to avoid arousing suspicion. Do this several weeks before starting your program so that no suspicion will be attached to your call and there will be no risk attached. With luck, the incident will be forgotten by the time the action starts. If there is any chance of your voice being recognized have a confederate whom you trust implicity make the call.

One good trick is to look in a swinger's magazine for homosexual prostitutes. These are usually advertised as "masseurs". Some of them make house calls. Send a few to his house. For an interesting variation, give one or two the address of his next door neighbor. If the "masseur" is effeminate in appearance or manner the neighbor will start to have horrible suspicions about the man next door when a gay boy rings his bell and asks for him.

Another good one is to have a confederate phone your target from a phone booth when he is home and ask for his wife. Your confederate should slur his speech as if he were drunk and say he is calling from a bar. A transistor radio playing loudly in the booth will help the effect. When the target asks what the call is about your friend can tell him that he saw his wife's name written on the toilet wall. If you have a number of friends you can trust not to shoot their mouths off you can pull this several times and have your target really believing that someone has been going around writing his wife's name and number on toilet walls. There is no point in making the rounds of bars and actually doing so, however, since harldy anyone calls numbers written on toilet walls. The multiplier effect would not work in this case.

If your target has an unlisted number it will significantly alter your plans. There are several ways to find out his number. One is to have a very good friend who works for the phone company do it for you. If you have no such friend you might be able to find it out from his place of work. If you work for the same company it is easier yet. If you don't you can phone his company one day when he is absent or out to lunch and say that you are the delivery supervisor for a piano dealer and that you would like to have his home number in order to find out when you can deliver the piano. You can tell the person to whom you are speaking that a clerk in your office forgot to type it on the order form and that you'd like to be able to check with the target's wife regarding the delivery. There are all sorts of variations possible on this theme. To give the situation some urgency, you can tell them that you have a load of concrete for his swimming pool or driveway and that you must get to his house before it sets. One of these stories will usually work, if you are calling a private company. If your target works for a government agency, however, don't even try this. They have a policy of not disclosing their employee's addresses or phone numbers and you won't get anything from them without a court order.

Another way to get his phone number if you know where he lives is to have a friend gain access to the house by posing as a salesman, census taker, repair man, etc. and reading it off the telephone dial.

Yet another way is for your confederate to pose as a salesman and tell the target's wife that he would like to demonstrate his product only when she and her husband are both home and that if she will give him the phone number he'll call back in the evening to arrange a time.

Additional Telephone Techniques

If you know that your target is being unfaithful to his wife you can have a confederate inform her by phone. One particularly effective way can be used if you know the time and place of the adulterous rendezvous:

"Hello, Mrs. Smith, Your husband told you he was going to be working late tonight but if you call his office you won't be able to get him. If you go to the XYZ Motel, however, you'll be able to see him if he and his roommate are not too busy."

You can also phone a famous crime figure, or a militant and denounce and insult him. This could prove to be at least embarrassing for the person whom you impersonate when making the call. A variation on this theme is discussed in the chapter on the use of the telegraph.

One additional resource the yellow pages lists is rental agencies. It is too easy to let your mind be channeled into looking only for companies with things to sell. Rental agencies will deliver appliances and furniture, as well as garden equipment and just about anything else you can buy.

Call Western Union

A remarkable number of things can be done by telegram. It is even easier to use Western Union in your plans than many other media because, 1. they are fast acting, and 2. they accept messages over the phone and charge them to your phone bill.

Some applications are:

Send Candygrams to all of your target's business associates and/or friends in his name and of course charge it to his phone bill. A nice twist it to charge it to his company's bill if he works for someone else. He will already be busy enough explaining phone calls, missing shipments, etc.

The day after he goes out of town, send a telegram to his boss saying something like this: "Have found better offer in Seattle. Sorry to leave you but it was an offer I couldn't refuse. Please send my final check to 1234 South 56th St. Seattle."

Send telegrams to various companies with whom he does business, cancelling shipments, ordering various items, or demanding payment of nonexistent shipments.

Send telegrams to his principle customers to inform them that the company has gone bankrupt. It will be doubly effective if you sign these "John Smith, President", even if he is only the janitor. In fact, giving him a false title will enhance the effect both on the accounts and on his boss, when he gets the bill.

If your target goes out of town on business you can send a wire to his hotel or the first company he visits, addressed to him and purportedly coming from his boss, telling him to come home immediately because his presence is urgently required.

Send wires changing or cancelling his hotel reservations.

If he owns his own business or is an officer of the company for which he works, send telegrams at night to some of the employees telling them not to report for work for whatever reason seems appropriate. (bankruptcy, vacation, layoff, fire, etc.)

At Christmas, send all of his employees a turkey by Western Union. One phone call will do it — Western Union will buy the turkeys, greeting cards, and will deliver them. They will also charge them to his phone bill.

It does not matter whether your target has an unlisted number or has his phone disconnected — you can still zap him by wire.

An additional technique you can use when sending telegrams is to send one in your target's name to the leader of a militant group in the area stating that you have evidence against him and will denounce him to the authorities the next day. This may provoke a reprisal.

20

Another way to foul him up by wire is to send a slanderous telegram to one of his friends or business associates. Some examples:

"Your employee Bill Jones is a homosexual. Suggest you fire him."

"Your employee Bill Jones has been spreading stories that you are a homosexual. Fire him."

"Saw your wife at the XYZ Motel with another man. Sorry to be the one to break the news."

"Your employee Bill Jones told me that he saw your wife at the XYZ motel with another man. Check it out for your own sake."

Green Stamps, Etc.

    An excellent way to use the multiplier effect is through classified ads. Most newpapers accept classified ads over the phone — you don't have to go to the office in person. This ensures your protection. They either bill the customer direct or charge it to his phone bill. This means it costs you only the price of the phone call to place a classified ad in your target's name.

The following trick was pulled very successfully several years ago. It tied up the target's phone for several days. This was particularly disturbing because it was a business phone. Place a classified ad that reads this way:

GREEN STAMPS FREE
Fifty thousand Green Stamps absolutely free.
Phone 123-4567

That's all. Callers will be tying up his phone day and night. If it is a business phone he is particularly vulnerable. He will miss important business calls and there is nothing he can do about it except to refuse to pay for the ad. A businessman cannot have his number changed to an unlisted one. He cannot have his phone temporarily disconnected. In any event you'll do that for him but that's in another chapter.

If you choose to list his home number in the Green Stamps ad it might be helpful to add another line: "Call after ten p.m." It will cost a bit more but you're not paying for it.

If your target is an employee rather than in business for himself you can hit him at work by listing his name in the ad: "Ask for Mr.——". After a few calls his boss will be asking him for an explanation. More explanation will be required if you have the newspaper bill his company.

There are many variations possible on this theme in order to run several ads at once and generate the maximum amount of calls to him. Keep in mind that if you hit his home phone he will have it changed or disconnected after a few days so you want to hit him as hard as possible while you have the chance. Free decals, samples, etc. are various possibilities. A little imagination will suggest more to you. Whatever you do keep in mind that it is important to avoid making the ad seem like a "Come-on" to a sales pitch. If that happens a lot fewer people will respond.

Another use of the classified ad should be held in reserve unitl your target has had his number disconnected or changed. It reads as follows:

WE PAY FOR RECYCLABLE CANS

"Bring your beer and soda cans and get ten cents apiece for them. Bring your bottles to be recycled and we will pay twenty-five cents each. Old tires one dollar."

This works best when you list a business address. There are two ways you can work it, however. One is to have people respond during business hours. Another is to state in the ad that if they come after business hours or on a weekend they are to deposit the recyclables in a designated spot (loading dock, parking lot, etc.) and leave a list of the items with their name and address in the mail slot or under the door and that a check would be mailed to them.

This method is also useful if your target is so disturbed by the harassment that he decides to go away for several days to get away from the delivery men, phone calls, etc. With the proper wording, you can arrange it so that when he comes home he will find his carport piled high with garbage.

Handbills and Circulars

There is one technique upon which you can fall back after your target has had his phone disconnected and the newspapers no longer take classified ads in his name. It requires access to a printing press or a duplicator. A Xerox will do fine.

The main idea is to print up advertisements for recyclables. For variety you can include a coupon at the bottom of the sheet for listing the contributor's name, address, the items brought in, their cash value (at ten cents per beer can this can add up to quite a bit) and whatever else seems appropriate to put on a coupon. Then print up a thousand of them and distribute them to every store in town. Put some in every public place you can think of. Try the public library. Don't ask permission — just lay a few on each table and counter. Put them by the cash register in luncheonettes. It's easy to get the owner's permission if you tell him it is for a worthy cause — ecology.

If you cannot duplicate these handbills yourself you will have to pay to have it done. It will cost quite a few dollars. A duplicating shop will do it for you at the least cost but don't make the mistake of going there yourself. Have a friend you can trust handle the transaction and have him pay for it in cash. Checks leave a trail and make it difficult to use an assumed name. You have to show a driver's license or other solid identification. Master Charge carries the same problem with it. Nobody questions cash on the barrelhead.

On the Job

One line of attack that you may be tempted to use is to cause trouble for your target on his job, if he is an employee and not self-employed. There are several ways of doing this.

One is to arrange for a series of phone calls to him on the job as outlined in a previous chapter.

Another way is to call his boss and tell him you are Mr. Smith from another company or an employment agency and that you are checking on how long he has worked there.

Yet another way is to call as a representative of a credit agency and ask if there are any garnishes on your target's pay. Or you could be checking his credit because your target is trying to purchase something beyond his means.

All of the above will create doubts about the target in the mind of his boss and this can lead to some very serious consequences for your target. Even if he manages to convince his boss that someone is trying to "get" him the target will still not have peace of mind. He will be gripped by fear of a nameless foe striking at him out of the shadows and disappearing before he can be seen. He will certainly lose a few nights' sleep over this, which is just as well, as he will then be up to answer the constantly ringing phone.

The more information you have about your target the better. If you know precisely what his job is, so much can be done based upon that information. You can impair him directly in his job.

For example, if he is a shipping clerk, you can phone several truckers and ask them to send a truck to pick up a shipment at his company. You could also call several truck lines and ask if they have shipments for his company. If they do, tell them to put them in storage and not to deliver them because (a) the plant is closing for vacation, or (b) the company has gone bankrupt. When you do this, make sure you give his name. As an extra twist, you might tell the official at the trucking company that if there are any questions he should call Mr.——, his boss.

House for Sale

One of the most productive ways of using the multiplier effect is put your target's house up for sale. This seems like a simple trick but it has so many subtleties and ramifications that analyzing them will take up a chapter.

Strangley enough the fact that your target does or does not own a house is of little importance to what you are trying to accomplish. If he does, so much the better — it enhances the effect. But if he does not, don't let that detail impede you. When you place the classified ad in the paper the people who will phone your target will not know before they phone that he lives only in an apartment.

The first step is to "case the joint" to see what sort of a house your target lives in. A good look at the real estate section of the paper will give you an idea of its market value. When you place the ad make sure that the asking price you insert is several thousand dollars below normal in order to attract the maximum number of people who will call. If the target does not own a house it's even easier. Pick any ad for a moderately low priced house out of the paper and drop the price by several thousand.

Do you want to include his phone number or his address in the ad? There are some pros and cons. If he doesn't have a phone (and some people in this country still don't) the choice is out of your hands. If he doesn't own a house except in your imagination then just list his phone. You might specify what time you wish prospective clients to call. In any event, when placing the ad charge it to his phone bill.

Another factor entering into your calculations is the timing. Are you placing the ad before or after you have his utilities cut off? This is important because if you include his phone number and at the same time arrange to have his phone disconnected it will be counterproductive. In that case it would be best to include only your target's address, thereby obliging interested parties to call on him personally. By this time he'll need people to tell his troubles to, anyway.

One effect of listing a house for sale in the paper is that real estate sales agents will be calling your target, or calling on him, as the case may be, in order to persuade him to list with their agency. The low price will insure that he gets their most prompt attention.

Magazine and Book Clubs

One of the most annoying things you can do to a person is to send in magazine and book club subscription cards in his name. This is not as threatening to his security as action on the job but rather it is like the drip-drip-drip of the Chinese water torture.

This requires some preparation. You must start collecting business reply cards some time in advance and in fact mail them four to six weeks before the main body of your plan goes into motion because it takes that length of time for the subscription to be processed and for the bills to be sent out.

There are several points in this procedure that require some discussion. First is the source of all these cards. Almost all magazines have subscription cards bound in somewhere. Most carry ads for other magazines and for book and record clubs. If you subscribe to a number of magazines there is no problem. If you don't, go to the library. You can probably snatch the cards out of the magazines without anyone objecting. A doctor's or dentist's office usually has a few magazines in the waiting room.

Make sure that what you send in are only postcards. They are handled by hordes of postal workers and you need not worry about fingerprints. When you fill them in be sure to turn the card upside down so that you are writing upside down and backwards. This is an old forger's trick to disguise handwriting. You won't have any worries about the cards being traced to you.

If there are subscription forms that require mailing in an envelope you will have to take the precaution of wearing plastic or rubber gloves.

You will probably want to avoid subscriptions that require that money be sent with the application, since your purpose is to harass your target, not give him a gift. The only exceptions to this are certain sexually oriented publications which could cause him considerable embarrassment if he gets them at home where his wife would see them or at work where his co-workers would see them. Particularly noteworthy are the gay magazines. However this could cost you quite a few dollars to do.

The effect of getting magazines and the bills for them can be very traumatic in this context as each will require a letter to the publisher explaining that he is the victim of a practical joke and requesting that the subscription be cancelled. The publisher may request that the magazines already received be mailed back. In the case of book or record clubs the return of the free introductory records or books will almost certainly be requested and this will cost the target more money and effort. He will be busy enough answering phone calls, sending back deliveries of pizza, food, and liquor, showing real estate agents the house, etc.

Cutting Off Utilities

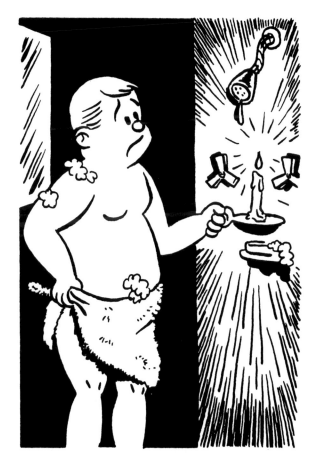

Imagine being home one day, taking a shower, when the flow of water stops. As you're scraping off the soap which you could not rinse off your wife comes to tell you that the gas furnace won't work. You go to have a look at it but the lights go out on you. Then you pick up the phone to call the utility companies but you don't even get a dial tone. At this point you might feel like a drink of beer from the refrigerator, which should still be cold, but if you were thinking of water, forget it. Also, what about all that food you've got in the freezer? It might go bad if you don't get the power turned back on soon.

That's what can happen to someone whose utilities are turned off simultaneously. You can do this to your target with just a few phone calls. It goes like this:

"Hello. This is Mr.—— of 1234 56th. St. We're going on vacation soon and we'd like to have the power (phone, water, gas) turned off on (date) and turned back on again on (date)."

Timing is very important here. It works best if all the utilities go out on the same day, in order to create the maximum inconvenience and dislocation. He won't be able to use his phone to have the other services turned back on. He'll have to use a pay phone or his neighbor's.

If you had one utility turned off each day, after the second day he would start to put two and two together and check with the other utilities and negate your effort.

The other critical aspect of timing is that the action against his utilities should not conflict with your other plans. His phone must be working in order for him to receive all those calls about the free Green Stamps and other important matters. Ideally, the utilities should be cut off before the other plans take effect. If he gets harassing phone calls before he may be calling the phone company himself to have his phone disconnected or his number changed to an unlisted one. He will then find out that it's already scheduled to be cut off and this may compromise the whole plan. Better to hit your target in his utilities first, before anything else (except for a few magazines that might trickle in early) and then when he gets everything going again, make him wish he'd never had his phone reconnected.

If your target does have his phone eventually disconnected, you must be flexible in your plans. For example, whatever classified ads you have not yet placed will have to be changed to show his address instead. If he's had his number changed to an unlisted one, there are ways of finding it out, as previously discussed.

It's a good idea to spot check his phone while your plan is running in order to determine if his phone is still working.

A quick call from a pay phone will do it. Check about once a day.

If you want to double his trouble, have the utilities turned off at his place of business simultaneously. If he is an employee, call the utility companies in his name but use the title vice-president, even if he is only the janitor. He will not be too happy at his sudden promotion and neither will his boss.

If he has his own business so much the better. He then will be facing double responsibility of getting things going again in both places at once. It is possible that a calm and resourceful person might be able to have all the utilities in both places turned back on by the end of the day but unfortunately for him compound problems usually snowball. By the end of the day the problems caused by the loss of the utilities will be piling up beyond his capacity to handle them. These may include customers who can't reach him, an account lost, production time lost, food spoiling in the freezer, etc.

In any event, if the timing is right, the next day will find the phone ringing off the hook and the target one day closer to an ulcer.

Playing Post Office

Most of us are dependent upon the Post Office in one way or another. We get and send personal mail and business mail. Disruption of this aspect of our daily existence can be very trying.

A word of caution, first. Interfering with the mail, robbing a mailbox, and opening other people's mail are federal crimes. The penalties are severe and the Postal Inspectors are the most efficient law officers in the country. Therefore the most important thing to remember if you want to get at your target through the mail is: "Don't break the law."

Sending someone magazine subscriptions is one way of getting at him through the use of the mails. Another way is to file phony change of address of cards for him. It is essential to use gloves and to write upside down when you do this, for obvious reasons.

Diverting his mail through a change of address card will be particularly effective if you list an address in another city as his new address. You can have his mail traveling across the country and, considering the state the Post Office is in these days, perhaps getting lost.

The consequences for your target will be more serious than they may seem at first sight. Not only will personal letters be diverted but also business mail, such as bills, bank statements, notices of payments, etc. The effect can be shattering if you do this to your target's business address. For a businessman, the loss of even one day's mail is a serious problem. He may be losing checks from his clients (that hits him in the breadbasket), legal papers, certificates, dividend checks, letters containing vital information such as price quotes, and many other types of mail which are vital to his business. There is even the happy possibility that he might not know that his mail is being diverted for several days. He might just think that nobody wrote to him that day. If he is a business man he will pick up on it much faster but he will still suffer since he has a lot more to lose.

A change of address card is a superb way to use the multiplier effect and make others do your work for you. An interesting variation on this idea, which can get the target's mail utterly lost, is the use of an accomodation address.

An accomodation address, sometimes called a secret address, is a service provided by some enterprising individuals to people who want to receive certain types of mail and yet keep their home addresses secret. These people often want to receive mail under an assumed name, and since the post office requires that you list your real name, the use of a post office box is out.

A careful look in most "swinger's" magazines will disclose some advertisements for these accomodation addresses.

40

The cost is usually indicated in the ad. There is usually a set fee per piece of mail.

If you file a change of address card to divert your target's mail to an accomodation address, and then arrange with them to remail it to a fictitious address, the mail can become utterly lost. If the fictitious address is in a foreign country and you instruct the accomodation service not to put a return address on the envelope in which they remail it, the chances of the mail either catching up with the addressee or being returned to the sender are infinitesimal.

This will cost you some dollars, particularly if you specify postage to a foreign country. Of course, you won't waste your money on air mail, as it is even better if the mail goes by ship, particularly a slow one.

When you hire the accomodation service in your target's name, it is best to pay them by a bank money order or cashier's check, also made out in his name, to prevent it from ever being traced to you.

If your target leaves town for several days, as discussed in the chapter on Green Stamps, it would be the perfect time to divert his mail. He will probably be so distraught that he will forget to file a hold mail notice with the post office and of course during his absence will be unaware that he is not getting mail. By the time he gets back quite a lot of his mail will be on the slow boat to Capetown.

The Neighbors

How do you mess your target up with his neighbors, just to add a little more misery to his life?

To begin with, when you buy him a subscription to a gay magazine you might put down his next-door neighbor's address instead of his. Even if the magazine comes in a plain brown wrapper the wrapper will sooner or later be torn, either accidentally by the delicate hands of the post office people or on purpose by a curious neighbor. In any event everybody knows what sort of publications are sent in a plain brown wrapper and when your target gets one handed to him by his neighbors, he knows that they know.

Another way to cause friction between him and his neighbor is to get out the yellow pages and order a truckload of manure or gravel to be dumped on his front lawn, only give his neighbor's address.

In some cities there are real estate agencies which deal mainly with Blacks. One way to exploit this fact is to phone one, impersonating your target, and invite a salesman (he will surely be Black) to come out to discuss selling the house. Give a neighbor's address. This of course only works if your target is Caucasian and lives in a lily white neighborhood. When it works, it works with a bang. The appearance of a Black real estate agent asking for your target will cause a lot of comment. Some people may even confront him, in which case he will naturally deny that he intends to sell his house to Blacks. Nobody will believe him.

Some of the regular magazine subscriptions can be purposely sent to people down the block. They may resent having to deliver his mail to him and in fact may not give him his magazines at all. They may even throw away the bill. If he does not pay a bill which has been sent to him it can reflect upon his credit rating and that can be explosive indeed.

Call boys or girls can be sent to his neighbor's address, as discussed in a previous chapter.

Hitting Below the Belt

In some instances it might seem to be a good idea to try to mess up his marriage. There are several ways to do this and none of them are sure to work. They will at least cause him some embarrassing moments and require him to make explanations to his wife, or her husband, as the case may be.

If your target is male, have a female accomplice whom his wife does not know phone his home and ask for him. If his wife answers, have her stammer that she has the wrong number and hang up. It might be best to do this when he's not at home but it doesn't really matter, since if he answers your accomplice can hang up without saying a word and try again later.

Sending him a birthday card and signing it with a woman's name and a few words of endearment can cause him an uncomfortable moment if his wife sees it.

One particularly nasty trick can be made to work if he regularly makes out of town trips. Write him a torrid love letter, seal it in an envelope and address it to him. Tear the seal open. Put the letter, still in its original envelope, in a larger envelope and address it to the postmaster of a city or town your target regularly visits. When the postmaster gets it, he will simply mail the enclosed letter. Time it so that it arrives at his home when he is out of town. Give his wife lots of time to read it and to think about it. A few sentences such as; "You keep telling me I'm better in bed than your wife but is it really true?" will give her a lot to think about.

Of course, a lot depends on how sound their marriage is and how much trust they have in each other. A healthy marriage will survive a lot of stress. Also, there is the ethical question of involving an innocent person, assuming that she is innocent. This does call for a lot of judgement, and if there is any doubt, it is best not to involve his family, particularly if there are children. They are always innocent.

Another useful way to hit your target below the belt is to have a confederate phone his home after he returns from an out of town trip. Your friend poses as the desk clerk of a motel in the city your target has visited and times his call to be sure that the target is not at home. When the wife answers he identifies himself and says something like this:

"After the two of you checked out the maid found some items of personal property while cleaning your room. Would you check to see if you left anything behind so that if they are yours we can send them to you?"

Murder, Inc.

It is a very uncomfortable thing to be suspected of murder, particularly when the police are not sure that the murder was committed on any particular date, so that no alibi is of any use.

You can arrange that situation for your target. The basic plan is this:

Rent a car similar to the one your target owns.

Make, with acrylic or some other glossy paint and a piece

of cardboard or metal, a license plate with his number on it.

Get an accomplice, male or female, someone whom you can trust absolutely and who is completely unknown to your target, his family, and friends.

Get a camera and a roll of color film.

One fine day, find a secluded spot out of the city. Pose your accomplice next to the car. Put the fake license plate over the car's real one and take a couple of shots, making sure that the plate number is visible in the picture. Next, pose your friend nude, not necessarily near the car. Next, tie your friend up and take some pictures in various poses. Next, take a large hunting or kitchen knife, break off the blade an inch from the hilt and scotch-tape it to your friend's body so that it looks as if it is sticking out of him or her. Put on a lot of red paint to simulate blood and to hide the tape. Finally dig up a mound of dirt that is about the size and shape of a grave. Put your friend's clothing next to it and take a picture. You can use a bit of imagination to vary the pictures to make them more interesting or incriminating, as the case may be.

Send the roll to be developed. Buy a mailer in a photo store. You don't have to give your real name when you buy a mailer. You fill it out at home, drop it in the mailbox, and the developed pictures will be mailed to the address you put on the tag.

Someone at the film laboratory will see those pictures. With the news media carrying stories recently about mass murderers, sex murderers, etc. it is a better than even chance that they'll call the police. Your target will have a lot of explaining to do.

High Risk Techniques

The following techniques involve moderate to high risk of discovery, as a rule. However, in certain circumstances, it will be possible to use these techniques at minimal risk, if you are careful.

If you have access to narcotics, you might try planting some in your target's car. An anonymous phone call to the police will do the rest.

The risk of a phone call to the police, which will surely

be taped, can be reduced greatly if you use a voice modulator, which in its simplest form is a piece of modelling plastic shaped to fit in the roof of your mouth. It fills in and changes the shape of your upper palate, thereby changing the sound of your voice. It will have no effect in your speech pattern, however. You'll have to be very careful what you say and how you say it, the best way to do this is to speak your message to the police into a tape recorder while assuming a regional or foreign accent. When you get results that you feel are different enough from your usual speech you can go to a phone booth and play the tape to the police. This should eliminate the risk of your voice being recognized by anyone. The voice modulator, combined with the distortion introduced by the tape recorder and the telephone, will make voiceprints useless. If you are going to be making a number of phone calls where your voice might be taped or recognized, a permanent voice modulator can be made using casting resin(epoxy).

Incidentally, the law in some states permits the police to not only impound, but to confiscate an automobile in which narcotics are found. This would add to your target's problems.

Planting contraband in your target's home is another possibility. One way is to have an accomplice gain access to the target's home while posing as a door to door salesman. If he can get in, he has a fifty-fifty chance of planting something.

If your target takes trips by air, an accomplice can follow him to the airport and in the crowd get close enough to him to drop a round or two of pistol ammunition in his pocket, or perhaps even a nasty looking switchblade. This is not as risky as it seems at first. If the target notices any furtive movement he'll of course check his wallet. When he finds nothing missing the incident will be closed. At the boarding area security check, however, it will be a different story. Your target will have a lot of explaining to do.

Another annoyance you can lay on for your target depends upon how good is your information about his movements. If you find out that he is booked on a flight,

50

you can phone the reservation desk and change his reservation to a later flight.

If you want to risk approaching his car and if it is usually left unlocked, you can put a pair of women's panties under the front seat in the hope his wife will find them. You could, for good measure, put a pack of condoms in the glove compartment. Some cigarette butts with lipstick on them in the ashtray will also build the chain of circumstantial evidence.

The Psychological Aspect

In this program of harassment the material losses you cause your target are only a part of the effect. More important is the psychological stresses to which he will be subjected — the climate of anxiety which you will create, the uncertainty as to where you will strike next. The cringing before the next blow is as important as the ton of manure on his front lawn. This introduces a new subtlety into your strategy. Your actions do not have to result in a physical act against your target.

This principle will also save you some time and trouble. Some of the stunts you pull will misfire but you can save the situation anyway. For example if you phone a real estate company to get a salesman to your target's house and you don't sound convincing enough you can, as soon as you sense that the person to whom you're speaking has doubts, ask him to call you back at your target's phone number. If you are trying to get a piano delivered to his house and are not quite making it you can ask for a call back. The threat of getting a piano delivered will shake up your target as much as the sight of the truck outside his front door. You can even plan it that way from the start. You probably realize that it is next to impossible to buy a piano or an organ by phone but knowing this you can nevertheless phone a piano dealer and ask the person who answers where your piano is and when it will be delivered. The person, of course, will be unable to find an order for it. Then you tell him or her that you don't want to tie up the phone while they check into it and ask that they call you back at your target's number as soon as they have the situation straightened out. They will and when your target hears that they are sorry but they can find no record of the order he will be agitated rather than relieved. If anything, he will be wondering what will be delivered to him rather than what will not.

If you call a gravel dealer to order ten tons of gravel to be delivered to your target and are told that no deliveries are made without a deposit you don't have to give up. You can say that the doorbell is ringing and ask that they call you back in a few minutes to give you a price on ten tons of crushed Vermont granite. This should be disturbing enough to your target to make it worthwhile.

In short if a plan misfires don't settle for a total loss. Make sure your target becomes aware of it and let him worry about it.

The Other Side of the Fence

What can your target do to defend himself against your harassment? What countermeasures can he take? It is important to be aware of the possible countermeasures in order to be able to forestall them and also to protect yourself against discovery and reprisals.

Most of the defenses are obvious. They are simple and forthright reactions to the threats as they appear. The target can be expected to make efforts to have spurious magazine subscriptions cancelled. He can ask the phone company for help. He can put a tape recorder on his line. As a last resort, he can have his phone changed or disconnected. These will do him little good since you can subscribe him to still more magazines, find out his new phone number, and strike at him through the mail or telegraph. Never under any circumstances call him from a phone that can be traced to you.

He can call the public utilities to have the services restored. He can eventually cancel a change of address card at the local post office but he won't be able to get back the diverted mail if you've handled it right. All of these responses will take up lots of his valuable time. Meanwhile he is vulnerable through other channels. The more you cause to happen to him in a certain period of time, the more difficulty he will have in coping with each threat. You will saturate his defenses.

If you hit him hard enough he may leave his job and move out of town. Life will have become intolerable for him and he will run.

However, it is good to remember that the best defense is a good offense. Your target will constantly be trying to figure out who is doing this to him so that he may retaliate. His retaliation, if he discovers you, may show some sophistication or may be directly violent. It will no doubt be very unpleasant for you and you may have to leave town.

Your target will surely have several suspects in mind. With a little imagination it should be possible to "frame" one of them for your activities. Keep in mind what the consequences may be for the one you frame and only do this if he is as equally deserving as your target.

Trouble with the Law

Two questions which you will be asking yourself all the time you're planning out a program against your target will be: What can the police do to me if they catch me? and "How can I avoid getting caught?"

Most of the actions suggested here are not even illegal. Some are misdemeanors. A couple, such as the one involving narcotics, are definitely felonies in most states. You can be sure that, for the most part, if your target complains to the police that someone is out to "get" him, they will see the matter as being out of their jurisdiction. After all what can the police do about someone sending a pizza to someone else's house? If the target is an influential person and the actions you take against him are extensive, they may provide him with a bodyguard if he can convince them that there is a threat to his life. This is very unlikely and even if it does happen it will not hamper you at all.

To avoid getting caught, it is necessary only to follow the simple rules of security discussed elsewhere in this manual. Keep in mind that the actions suggested are designed to be untraceable to you and that the police's manpower and resources are very limited. This last point requires some discussion.

Anyone who takes a careful look at a real police department rather than at the TV cops sees that they are overworked, understaffed, and do not solve most of the crimes reported to them. A quick look at the annual FBI report for 1973 shows that the percentage of cases "cleared by arrest" stands at 79 percent for murder and goes down to under 20 percent for lesser crimes such as burglary. The more violent the crime, the more effort is put into solving it: the less violent, the more is the tendency to put it into the file along with all the others and get to it when time permits. There is a tendency in some police departments to persuade suspects to confess to crimes they did not commit, in order to get them off the books and to pad the clearance rate. The police make a "deal". The suspect confesses and in return gets a reduced and perhaps a suspended sentence. This is what often accounts for the spectacle of disproportionally light sentences being handed out for relatively serious crimes.

The police's way of working is also germane to this discussion. Rarely in real life, as contrasted to the TV cops, are the latest advances in science brought to bear upon the solution of the crime. Rarely are entire teams of detectives assigned to a case. The police don't have the manpower to drop everything and intensively investigate any but the most serious crimes. An ordinary murderer will typically have two detectives assigned to seeking him. These two detectives usually have a caseload of other murders upon which they are working at the same time. Only in the case of a cop-killer or a bizarre sex murder is the full manpower of a police department brought to bear upon the problem. To sum up, your target's complaint, even if accepted by the police, will have to wait its turn at the end of a very long line.

The way in which the police solve cases is important to consider. Most of the time, it is done by informants. These are people who either get paid for their information or are under suspicion themselves and try to make a "deal" with the police in order to obtain lenient treatment. Surveillance, telephone taps and traces, and other exotic means of detection are rarely used because they are expensive, both in equipment and manpower, and because most of the time they cannot be used in court. Consider that it takes at least three men to maintain a round-the-clock tap on a particular telephone and that it takes additional men to trace a particular call, and yet more men to speed to the scene and make an arrest and you can see how much of a problem a telephone surveillance is. For a police department to put that much effort into solving a crime which most likely is only a misdemeanor and which does not involve violence, is unthinkable when you consider the great number of violent crimes being committed very day.

The myth of your handwriting being traced by checking Army records, old school records, etc., collapses when you consider the huge manpower effort that it would involve. In any event, the risk is relatively easy to avoid.

Finally, the probability of the case holding up in court is very, very poor. The FBI statistics show that only a fraction of the crimes cleared by arrests conclude with a successful prosecution. What the police know and what they can prove in court are obviously two different things.

The greatest danger to you is not from the police but from your target. If he comes to suspect you, that suspcion does not have to stand up in court for him to begin his own retaliatory program of harassment. Therefore it is very important to follow the security measures outlined in this manual. Do not have any personal contact with your target: do not talk about your plans to anyone who does not need to know; and allow enough time to elapse in order to give your target time to forget about you. By following these simple rules you will not be trusting to just luck but will be actively safeguarding your own security.

Your Target Is Vulnerable

The strategy of harassment is built on the premise that most people in twentieth century America are vulnerable to serious disruption of their lives through clever manipulations of society's own institutions. They are vulnerable because everyday life for almost everyone is so complex and because of the interdependency upon which we must rely for even the barest necessities. Everyday life is so delicately balanced for most of us that one thing or another is almost constantly going wrong even without outside interference. Power failures and subway strikes, delayed or lost mail are so common that we almost consider them as normal occurences. Most of the technological aids of the twentieth century are essentially two-sided in that they can be helpful or harmful. A credit card is a great convenience but if you lost yours you may find that someone else has been charging purchases to your account. The telephone, which can be found in almost everyone's home, can be either an extremely useful gadget or an instrument of evil. The same instrument that enables you to speak with someone across the continent can also bring you sales solicitations, crank calls, or wrong number calls at three o'clock in the morning.

Today, when many feel that they live in a country in which people enjoy greater freedom than most other people on earth, we are more and more becoming trapped by the constraints of the twentieth century industrial society. We really have less day-to-day freedom than our grandparents did. We have more obligations to meet, taxes to pay, bills and mortages to pay; there are more laws which we must obey than ever before. We have to report to jobs that are more complex and require more skills than ever before and yet we are increasingly insecure in those jobs. Our lifestyles are more threatened and we have fewer defenses than ever before.

Who is most vulnerable? Everyone except the very poor and very rich — the poor because they have little to lose. They often do not have phones or cars and many do not even have jobs. Few own their own homes. It is next to impossible to have anything delivered to a ghetto address.

The very rich are well insulated from the hassles of the everyday world. They have secretaries to answer their mail and other employees to answer the phone and the doorbell. The usual harassment measures will only fall upon the employees, not the target himself.

Nevertheless, there are still some measures that can be taken against someone who is at one of the extremes of the economic spectrum. The task requires more intelligent planning, better information, and the plan must be tailored to the individual case.

Some of the rich are vulnerable because their activities are publicized. They also do a lot more travelling than most other people. This makes them especially prone to having their reservations cancelled by spurious telegrams, to cite but one possibility.

Planning It Out

As you have seen from the preceeding chapters, everyone is vulnerable to harassment in may ways. It is possible, by careful planning and a moderate amount of effort, to make life absolutely miserable for the one whom you select to harass.

One of the first things you must consider in making your plan is how much are you prepared to spend, in both money and time. The main reason that harassment is not used much more than it is, is that most people do not go about it systematically and soon find themselves spending so much time, with so little results in proportion, that they soon get tired of it and give up. You can see, however, that you can get big results from little effort if you approach the problem in the right way.

Money is another problem. Most of the techniques outlined here cost very little to apply; the cost of a few phone calls, a couple of dollars in postage. Some can cost a lot more; the cost of renting a car, the service of an accomodation address. Decide in advance what you can afford.

Using the multiplier effect is the key to getting maximum results with a minimum of effort. The second most important thing is to have the various phases of your plan properly coordinated so that they do not conflict with each other and cancel each other out. You can easily see that it makes no sense to have your target's phone service cut off on the same day that your classified ad offering green stamps appears in the paper. Proper timing is all-important.

Lead times are also considered. It takes various amounts of time to put the various phases of your plan into effect. A change of address card takes a couple of days: magazine subscriptions take weeks: a delivery of booze or flowers takes only minutes between the time you place the call and the delivery itself. Lay out these different lead times on your chart. See how they tie in with each other.

Select the date on which you want your program to begin. Call it D-Day. You can see that your preparations may have to begin weeks ahead of D-Day. This is just as well because you don't want to be choked with more work on the last few days before the big day.

You do have a job to keep: you do have personal commitments to attend. You can't tie up your time for several days straight. Proper planning will smooth out your workload.

Selecting the things you want to do to your target is important. Not every phase can be applied to everyone. If your target is unmarried, or does not own a car, it will limit your choices somewhat. Whatever you do, don't try to do too much at one time. Time is on your side. You can always hit him with more later on.

There is only one exception to this rule. It is usually most effective to cut off his phone, utilities, and mail, both at home and at work, on the same day. That way he will be saturated and will be least able to take effective measures to restore these vital functions. In fact, if his phone and utilities go out on him all at once he probably won't even notice that he's not getting any mail for a day or two, thereby increasing the damage.

There is a sample chart on the next page. It will give you a general idea of how to plan your program.

One final word: keep your plan a secret. Don't tell anyone at all about it unless that person needs to know because he or she is your accomplice in some phase of it. People do gossip. The word might get back to your target and then you will have just as many problems as he does. Remember that he can do the same things to you.

D - DAY

-60 -30 -10 -5 -0- +1 +2 +3 +4 +5 +10 +15 +20 +30 +45

Send in magazine subscription cards

Phone the utilities to have his services cut off on D-Day.

Send in a change of address card.

Arrange for an accomodation address to forward his mail outer Mongolia.

Phone in the classified ads.

Have his car towed away.

Start using job action against him.

Call the real estate agents.

Have booze and flowers delivered.

Send him ten pizzas for supper.

Have manure dumped on his lawn.

Send a gravel truck to his neighbor's house.

Have a Pharmacy deliver asprin He'll need them!!

Send some Chinese food.

THE "PLAN"

Notes on Sources

Most ideas for harassment come from the yellow pages. This is your best source of ideas in one volume. A little imagination can contribute more.

Another source of ideas is the book "The Compleat Practical Joker" by H. Allen Smith. Yes, that is the way "compleat" is spelled in the title. This book is an exhaustive list of practical jokes which have been pulled successfully by various people and the only drawback is that most of the stunts listed have to be done in person. They require some personal contact and this is exactly what you must avoid. With a little imagination some of the ideas can be adapted to work by remote control and given a vicious twist — it's up to you.

There are several books on the Watergate affair which touch upon the activities of Donald Segretti, the principal character in the harassment program directed against the Democratic candidates. The one by Chester, MacCrystal, Aris, and Shawcross is an excellent one.

The classified ads in Mechanix Illustrated, Popular Science, Popular Mechanics, and various men's magazines are a gold mine of accomodation address services. There are many, many, of them all over the country and if you want to spend the money the prospect of routing your target's mail through several of them is very attractive. It makes the mail really untraceable and eliminates any chance of a cablegram to the Capetown postal authorities getting the mail back.

A Quick Review of Strategy

    The basic idea is to cause your enemy, or target, more harassment and discomfort than he has caused you, and to do this without being discovered. A few fundamental principles will help you to plan and carry out a successful campaign of harassment:

1. Get as much information as possible on your target before you make your first move. The need for some basic

data is obvious; name, address, type of car he drives, employment, time schedule, amd marial status. Not so obvious but very helpful in some circumstances is other information, such as: his exact position in his company, where he goes on vacation or business trips, hobbies, and whatever guilty secrets he has.

2. Prepare your plan carefully before you make the first move. Put it in writing. Make a chart, as described in the first volume of Harassment, as a guide to action. This will enable you to carry out your plan without any aspects of it conflicting. You would not want, for example, to have his phone service cut off just as he is about to get a series of annoying phone calls.

3. Avoid all personal contact with your target, if possible. You don't want to be recognized as the driving force behind his problems. Unless you work with him, for him, or are his neighbor, stay away from him.

4. Use the multiplier effect as much as possible. Let others do the work for you. Arrange for others to call him at all hours of the day or night, rather than staying up yourself to do it. Have others deliver packages or trash to him. Specific guidelines on how to do this are in both this book and the first volume.

Luck

Few people appreciate what a large part pure luck plays in their lives, preferring to believe that you make your own luck or something of the sort. Yet a lot of events are determined by luck, much more than it is expedient to admit. A distinguished career can be cut short by a traffic accident in which someone else's brakes happen to pick that moment to fail. Or an investor with a lot of money happens to meet a man with a marketable idea but no capital.

The same thing can happen with harassment. Sometimes luck can work for you, and you must be prepared to recognize it if it happens, and exploit it fully.

For example, your target may misplace his wallet. You find it. This can be a gold mine of opportunities. At the very least, a lost wallet that is not returned is a great annoyance in our Twentieth Century society. The credit cards that must be replaced, the driver's license and various other official documents that are lost can tie up a lot of your target's time. You can cause your target even more annoyance by making purchases with his credit cards (act fast, before they can be put on the hot list) and having them delivered to his home or business. You don't have to be physically present to do this, as many concerns will accept phone orders.

Bits of paper with addresses and phone numbers on them may reveal all sorts of damaging information about your target. He may be carrying his girlfriend's number, which can be very interesting if he is married.

You may find out some damaging information about your target by luck alone. You may know somebody who knows something which, when put together with something else that you know, can open up your target to another devastating action. Or something may happen to your target which may make him vulnerable to some action on your part. For example, if he is under indictment for a business fraud, and this makes the front page of the paper, you can spend a rewarding afternoon with a telephone calling up the media, impersonating your target, and making all sorts of threats and obscene statements in his name. You can generate so much flak for him that he will wonder what hit him.

Often, a bit of luck will present you with an opportunity to do extensive damage to your target, much more than you could have done by other means. You must be alert to recognize such an opportunity if it presents itself, and to act on it immediately. You have to be able to think on your feet and to think fast. It is impossible to foresee luck, but it is possible to grab it when you see it and make it work for you.

The Need for Caution

When you embark upon a program of harassment you have to do so carefully. Your purpose is to cause your target grief, not yourself. You must be bold, but not reckless.

It has been said that "fortune favors the brave". For those who like these maxims there is also: "Discretion is the better part of valor". Unless you feel that you are engaged in a macho contest with your target you must be cautious and discreet. If you feel that it is a question of your manliness versus his, just challenge him to a duel and get it over with.

The central fact is that if your target discovers who is at the root of all the misfortunes which are falling upon him like an avalanche, he can do the same to you, or worse. If your target is a large corporation, for example, it can hit you with injunctions and civil suits and make them stick. They might even be successful at instituting criminal proceedings against you, as they have many lawyers on their staffs and they are fully prepared to use the law to defend what they see as their interests. Then you will find out that the government can move fast when a large corporation demands action. The police and prosecutor, whom you thought were in a catatonic stupor when you asked for help, will suddenly wake up and land on you with both feet.

You must be cautious and you can afford to. Time is on your side. Unless your target is dying of a terminal illness you can proceed slowly and carefully, planning each move so that there is no wasted motion and you get the best use out of your limited resources.

It is important not to tip your hand by acting impulsively. Doing so will alert your target and cause him to close off an avenue of approach that you could have used later with more effect. It is important not to pull your punches. It is important to hit him as hard as possible each time, or you will be wasting your effort.

If you choose an accomplice, be careful. It is better to be forced to act alone than to have as co-conspirator someone who cannot be trusted and who will do you more harm than good in the long run.

Discretion is important after it is all over, too. You might be tempted to brag to your friends and acquaintances about how you "got" someone who did you dirty, but keep your mouth shut. The fact is that the effect on your target will be enhanced if he never finds out who did it to him, and while you may feel that you can trust your friends, one of them might tell someone who will go running to your target with the information.

It is also important not to get carried away so much that you hurt innocent people. In the rush of enthusiasm as you see your moves working to make your target's life hell, it is easy to get careless and to do things that will also fall upon innocent people around him. For example, it is nice to find a way to put a powerful laxative in his coffee, but what if someone else drinks it too? That is a risk that you must judge carefully.

Yet other reasons for exercising caution are that you do not want to give the opportunity for a psychological release, even if all he can do is to call you names.

If your target is as bad as you think he is, there is a great possibility that someone else may have already done something to him in retaliation for a wrong, and that he may already be on his guard. If you are unaware of this, and you go ahead without planning for it, you might run into more trouble than you can handle. If, for example, you decide to take the risk of going onto his property one night you might find that he has installed an ultrasonic alarm because someone else did it to him last year.

Why take any risk at all? Your purpose is to do a job on him, not to prove how brave you are. Your purpose will best be served if you can remain unobserved and undetected throughout, while your target frets and worries about who is doing these terrible things to him. The guiltier his conscience is the more he will suffer.

Getting Information about Your Target

The more you know about your target the more levers you have to make his life miserable. Accurate information is an absolute prerequisite before you can make any plan.

The usual ways of findings out things about your target will work up to a point. You can get his phone number and address from the phone book in most cases. You can find out other things about him through personal acquaintance. Sometimes your target will be a comparative stranger with an unlisted number. What then?

There is a way, apart from hiring a private detective, but it will cost you a little money. The total cost, however, will still be less than the cost of a private eye.

This method is based on the fact that people will give all sorts of information about themselves when they apply for a job. Often they will abjectly answer questions that their prospective employer has no business asking.

Run a classified ad for your target's job category. Mention a high rate of pay as a further inducement to persuade him to respond. Ask for resumés to be sent to a box number. If you already have a post office box you're ahead by one step. If not, rent one. If you regularly scan the employment ads in your local paper you know that many companies run "blind" ads, that is, ads which do not identify the company but just list a box number.

The wording of the ad is important, as it will determine to an extent what information you will get. Normally a resumé will contain the applicant's name, address, family listing, job history, and educational background. If you want other information you'd better ask for it. Some possible wordings are as follows:

"Include salary history and requirements" will tell you what he earns.

"Transportation a must. Include details of transportation" will usually get you his car make, if you don't already know it.

"Include Social Security number and bank references in your resumé". You can make good use of this information if you decide to send in official forms in your target's name.

"Personal references required with resumé". This will get you the names of some of his friends, which can be useful if you decide to pull some of the stunts which will alienate him from his friends and neighbors.

There is no way to guarantee that he will answer the ad, of course, but you might help things along, if you work with him, by showing him the ad, or if that seems unlikely, leaving the classified section open on his desk. That can cause him a problem if the boss walks by and sees the paper open to the help wanted section. Another way is to send him a clipping of the ad in the mail, with an unsigned note saying that he might be interested in the ad. He can only assume that a friend sent it and forgot to sign his name: after all, who else would send him a job ad?

If and when you get his resumé in your box you will have part of the information that you can glean with the method. The follow-up is very important and can get you even more than you expect, or need. Phoning companies at which he worked can get you a gold mine of information about your target that he might not have put in his resumé.

Many companies will not give out any information about present or past employees over the phone. This will obstruct you but you can work around it. It is easy to have a letterhead printed up with your box number as the mailing address. A letter from "B.J. Snodgrass," of "B.J. Snodgrass & Co., Consulting Engineers" will often get you a reply, though usually the information supplied will be limited to a verification that your target worked there from one date to another and a general statement that his performance was satisfactory.

Your target's resumé might list fishing as one of his hobbies, as a dry fact, but if you can speak with someone who likes to talk you can fill out the picture a lot more. That someone might tell you that he and the target once went fishing up at the lake, where the target has a summer home. You can use that information in several ways, such as having a woman leave a message for him that she won't be able to meet him up at the lake that weekend.

His resumé might mention that he does free-lance work without going into details, but a phone call might get you the information that he is moonlighting for a company that is a competitor of the one for which he works now (luck again), a fact that might interest his present employer very much if brought to his attention. Send his boss a letter about it. Mention dates, places, and all the specific information that you have. You don't have to worry about an anonymous

81

letter being thrown into the wastebasket—sign one of his friend's name to it.

The fake employment ad can bring you information other ways too. You are likely to get several replies to the ad. People who are in the same line of work often know each other. In fact, you might get a reply from someone who worked for the same company as did your target at the same time. You can call such a person on the telephone under the pretext of interviewing him for the job and ask him questions about your target. You can be perfectly frank and say that you received an application from him, too, and are checking him out as well. The conversation might go like this:

"Oh, by the way, I see that you worked at the ABC Company three years ago. Did you know Joe Blow?"

"Yes, I did. He worked in the XYZ Department just down the hall".

"What sort of a person was he?"

"Oh, a pretty good guy, I guess. I've been over to his house with my wife for dinner several times. Is he applying for the job, too?"

"Yes he is. In fact, I know him too, but mainly by reputation. He's trying to get another job now because they found out he's gay where he works now. That business with the teen-ager last month, but well, you know about that."

"No, I had no idea. What happened?"

"Well, I don't want to talk about it, the poor guy's had a rough enough time over it. That came right after his wife had the abortion, too."

Get the idea? You can plant some nasty time bombs this way, ruining his reputation by slander with absolutely no risk to yourself.

Involving Others

There are two ways to involve others in your campaign of harassment; as accomplices and as co-targets.

Not having any accomplices may cramp your style. There are tricks that you cannot pull off alone: there are those which require two people working in tandem. Sometimes you need help in an auxiliary task. Then you need an accomplice or two.

There are two kinds of accomplices; willing and unwitting. If you decide that you need a willing accomplice, choose him or her carefully. You want someone with good judgment and common sense, someone who does not think it is all a joke and gets careless. You want someone with enough emotional maturity that he or she will not brag about it in a bar. That kind of talk has a way of getting back to the wrong ears, where it could do you a lot of harm.

Preferably, you should choose an accomplice who has a personal stake in the matter. If your target is your former employer who has treated you unfairly, there may well be other employees or ex-employees who have their own reasons for revenge. If your target is a car dealer who shafted you, then he probably shafted a lot of other people too, and one of those people may well be a friend or acquaintance of yours who will eagerly go along with your plans.

The sort of person who deserves to be harassed is usually the sort who makes enemies in droves, not an otherwise harmless individual who had a personality clash with one person. The target is usually a vicious, exploitative, and abrasive person who has anatgonized many besides yourself. It should not be too hard to find an ally.

If you can't find an ally, you will have to use unwitting accomplices. Such can be the postman who delivers an envelope for you. Another might be a messenger service. Yet another might be a real-estate agent who goes to your target's house when you put it up for sale. These are innocent people and you must be careful not to expose them to any danger.

Sometimes you can make an unwitting accomplice out of someone who fits into the category of co-target. It is a very gratifying feeling to set the wolves at each other's throats. Many of the chapters in this volume will suggest ways to do this.

Yet another way in which you can involve others is as co-victims. Often, there is some risk to innocent people and this is why you will not want to do some things that would be very effective in causing your target distress. For example, cutting the brake lines on his car might well involve innocent people in an accident. He might lend the car to someone else or injure or kill someone when his brakes fail. Chemical additives to his food or drink are risky when there are others living at the same address.

There are always a few who will say: "The innocent must suffer along with the guilty" but such an attitude is neither Christian nor charitable and it puts that person in the same category as the bad guy he is harassing. It is quite possible to strike selectively at your target, and to strike hard without catching everyone else in the crossfire. If you use your wits and follow the suggestions outlined in this book, you will be able to adapt and shape your plans so that your target will catch all the flak, with little or no fallout on his family or friends.

Finally, there is a category of people who can be manipulated to do the dirty work and take the risk without any qualms of conscience. These are the outcasts: Career criminals, dopers, bikers, deviates of all sorts. Like it or not, we view these people as beyond the pale and deserving of anything that happens to them. Everybody, no matter how liberal or broad-minded he thinks he is, has certain categories in his mind which he considers as sorry specimens of the human race and deserving of less consideration than other people.

These people may be innocent of whatever it is your target has done to you but to you they are still outcasts, apart from polite or civilized society and if they come to grief one way or another you are not going to care very much. A derelict who freezes to death in the park one night does not cause much of a ripple in the lives of the other residents of the city. A professional tough guy who is injured in an altercation with your target will not cause you to weep for him. These people are innocent and yet less than innocent. The choice and the moral judgment are yours.

Typewriter Tricks

You will find that a typewriter can be very useful to you in a campaign of harassment. Your first step will be to procure a typewriter than cannot be traced to you and which is expendable so that you can dispose of it afterwards.

A good place to get such a typewriter is at a garage sale or a thrift store. Whatever the case, there are two things to watch: make sure it is a machine which types in PICA type, which is larger, for legibility, and you don't want to use a check or a credit card to pay for the machine, as this leaves a paperwork trail which will lead right to your door. The machine need not be in really good shape for what you want. It should be cheap, so that you will not feel too badly about dumping it in the river after you're through with it.

A typewriter is a good way to avoid using your own handwriting when you have to make a piece of written communication, such as a poster or filling out a subscription coupon. You can use it to type threatening letters in your target's name. You can use it to make posters.

The easiest and fastest way to make a poster, and also the cheapest, is to type it out in capital letters on your typewriter. Take it to a coin-operated copy machine for extra copies. You have to be careful here, choosing a machine that is in a location with low traffic, so that nobody will see what you are doing. When making posters, a useful trick is to type the master copy with everything except your target's house number. You can fill this in individually on each one later, putting a different number on each one, to make sure his neighbors get their share of the traffic. A bonus feature of this trick is that the neighbors will be on his case for being so stupid as to put down the wrong address on the posters. They will resent being disturbed by bikers or perverts going to his party or meeting.

Some of the tricks you can pull with a typewriter in your program of harassment are frankly illegal, so you want to be sure that you do not use your own typewriter for them. In that regard, you will want to dispose of the machine as soon as possible after the successful conclusion of your campaign. If you have more than one target, do not hesitate to buy another typewriter for that purpose exclusively. If any of these activities come to the attention of the police they will certainly be comparing modus operandi and any physical evidence, such as typewritten material. Any link between two targets of harassment may lead them to your door by a process of elimination, and even if you have gotten rid of the evidence down the nearest sewer drain, just being on someone's suspect list can be very uncomfortable.

Tricks with the Telephone

The telephone can be a great convenience in our society or it can be an instrument of evil. Many, many techniques of harassment start with a phone call. Some of them are the following:

If your target is married, have a female accomplice call him at home, preferably when you know he will not be home, so that his wife will pick up the phone. It is very easy to generate suspicion this way, particularly if your accomplice does not leave a name and has a slight flair for acting.

If your target is female, a male accomplice can do the same thing. A variation on the theme can be to tell the husband that he (the accomplice) feels sorry for him, that his wife is no good in bed anyway, and that he is calling it off for this reason.

Whether your target is single or married, if he is male, you can have an accomplice who can put on an effeminate voice call him at work. Do this a few times and you will generate some dark suspicions about him in the minds of his fellow workers. A use of the multiplier effect here would be to generate such calls to your targets by putting an ad in a gay swingers' magazine with his phone number included.

The best results will be obtained, of course, if the phone calls come when your target is not at work. If he is out to lunch, or if his job takes him out of the plant for hours at a time, (delivery work, salesman, etc.) he is particularly vulnerable to tactics such as these. The effect can be enhanced if the caller leaves a message such as "Meet me at _____ (the name of a gay bar) after work."

Another possibility is to have an accomplice phone your target, telling him that he is the manager of a well-known restaurant in the area, and that as a promotional measure he is invited to a free dinner for himself, his wife, and a couple of guests. If your target does not double check on this one, and if the restaurant is not one where you normally phone for reservations, he can show up ready for dinner and maybe even have a meal before the awful truth is revealed.

Variations on the free meal theme are endless. Your accomplice can say that he is the manager of a theater, an amusement park, or any consumer service business. If a real promotional program is being made at the time in your area, (luck) you can take advantage of it and have your accomplice make a spurious phone call to your target. If a hotel advertises that it is offering waterbeds in a limited number of rooms, for example, (luck again) you can call up your target to tell him that you are giving him a free night in a waterbed-

90

equipped room for himself and his wife or girlfriend. If he accepts, you or your accomplice can tell him that the reservation will be waiting for him. Then, of course, you must do your homework and actually phone in the reservation to the hotel, because it will be more awkward and embarrassing for your target if he actually uses their services and runs up a bill than if he finds out it is spurious before he even checks in.

An additional variation on this theme can be run if your target is a company or a man who owns a business that normally uses hotel services and has an account at a hotel. Then you can have others use the services and have them billed to the company. It takes some phoning around but it can be done.

Impersonating your target on the phone can be very rewarding at times, and even more so if you can do it in certain circumstances of special knowledge. For example, if you know that he owes a lot of money and you know who one of his creditors is, say a bank or a large company, you can phone them up and be very threatening and abusive. This works only if the person to whom you are speaking does not know him personally and would not recognize his voice.

If you know that your target is having a problem with his taxes, a phone call to the relevant bureaucracy will do wonders.

If your target is going through a divorce action and if you know who his wife's lawyer is, a phone call can do a lot. The chances are that the lawyer will not know your target's telephone voice. If he does, you can call when he is out and speak to a secretary or to a partner. Most lawyers spend a good amount of time out of the office, say in court, and most have partners. The exact content of the telephone "conversation" will be determined by your target's situation and what you know of it (luck again) but if you do it right you can get your target in a lot of hot water. For example:

"I'll be damned if I'll let that %$&** broad have the house! I'll burn it down first! In fact, if I don't hear from her by three o'clock, I'm going to go over tonight with five gallons of gasoline and torch it myself."

"I want custody of the kids. You shyster, you &(%$$&&,

if you don't drop that demand I'm coming over there and beat the shit out of you!"

"That's not her car. I don't care if you have a court order. If she comes over here to get it I'm going to be here with a shotgun and I'm going to blow her head off! Then I'll take care of you, too."

The possibilities are endless. You can cause your target so much mischief with the judicious use of the telephone that you will make his life unbearable. You are limited only by your imagination.

A Man's Home Is His Castle

An excellent way to harass someone is to hit him right where he lives—literally.

Apart from having all sorts of goods and services sent to his house, you can have people visit him in droves. One good way to do this is to put up posters inviting people to an open house at his address. It gets more interesting if you put the posters up on your city's skid row and include the caption: "All you can drink." The occasion can be everything— Christmas, Halloween, the Fourth of July. Each occasion suggests its own special variation.

For Halloween, a costume party can be the event. For New Year's Eve, a boozy bash; only make sure that your target will be at home for this one. It will do no good if he's going to someone else's party. If he is having one of his own, a few dozen unexpected guests can cause him some concern, particularly because some of them may already be in there and mingling with the legitimate guests by the time your target realizes that anything is wrong.

For Veteran's Day, a small poster in every bar you can find, inviting all veterans to a "Special Recognition Party" at your target's house will do the trick.

For the Fourth of July a poster on the local Salvation Army bulletin board will attract all sorts of people. If you want to make it more interesting, put a poster where a local motorcycle gang hangs out.

If there is a local motorcycle gang in your area with a reputation for nasties, a poster announcing a motorcycle beauty contest, with a prize for the best looking bike and your target as the judge, will make it very hot for him and cause him much distress.

An advertisement in your local paper announcing the formation of a new organization for ex-convicts and having its first meeting at your target's address will generate some excitement on his block, particularly if you word it so that he is identified as an ex-con himself. If you put a notice up on the bulletin board in the local parole and probation office, you will reach the people you need.

The same tactic can be used with other out-groups as the theme. Homosexuals, alcoholics, and child molesters can all be invited to a meeting at his house.

If you live in a large city where the conditions are right and you have enough nerve, you can go into the local gay bars and put up posters announcing a "drag ball" at his house. For those not familiar with the term, a "drag ball' is an affair involving people who dress in the clothing of the opposite sex. The nerve comes in when you go into a gay bar and ask for permission to put up the poster. You cannot usually furtively sneak in and staple it to the nearest wall. Establishing a rapport with the bartender or owner of the establishment can be enough to tax the fortitude of the strongest among us, but the results can be worth it.

If you want to twist the knife a little more, on the posters in a dozen different places you can make sure a dozen different neighbors are made aware of what sort of people your target is inviting to his home.

A variation which will cost you a little money is to go down to the local skid row and recruit some of the bums you find there to come to your target's house to sing Christmas carols on his lawn. If it is Christmas that is fine, but if it is not, you will have to be inventive. You can tell them that the target has a child dying of leukemia and that he is having Christmas early for him or her this year. To assure their attendance, it is a good idea to give each bum a couple of dollars each when you ask him to come, and to tell him that he will get another five or ten when he finishes singing. You may easily wind up spending twenty, fifty, or even a hundred bucks, but if you are determined enough on revenge it will be worth it to you.

I Read It in the Paper

Newspaper ads are a commonly suggested and frequently used method of sending some harassment in your target's direction.

The possibilities are very wide and your imagination will be your best guide. There are some limitations, though, and you should be aware of them before you start. I have worked for several newspapers and am familiar with the problems.

There are basically two types of ads that newspapers run, classified and display ads. The classified ads have only type in them, are usually very small, and are run in columns along with other ads of the same classification.

Display ads are the big ones with pictures run by department stores and other businesses, and they may be any size, up to a full page.

Classified ads are accepted by telephone, and usually run without advance payment or a credit check, as there are so many and their dollar value per ad is so low that it would be uneconomical to fully check out each one. The operators taking the ads rely upon common sense and a "gut feeling" to separate the real ones from the spurious ones. If the ad sounds reasonable, and is worded pretty much like the other ones, you should have no trouble running it and having your target billed for it.

Display ads are another matter. You can't just phone in and order a full-page or half-page ad. You have to turn in a layout and artwork, as well as the wording. If you are not an established account, you may be asked to pay in advance. You can't usually do it by phone. An ad salesman, called an "account executive" will come out to see you. There will be personal contact, just what you most want to avoid, for when the ship hits the sand you will be remembered.

It is difficult, if not impossible, for you to phone in a display ad order and to say that you'll mail the layout and artwork, for if you try to impersonate an established account you will find that the ad salesman will know you are a fake, as he deals with the client directly and knows his voice. Also, many publications, not only newspapers, require what is called an insertion order before running any ad. That is a purchase order for the ad specifying where and when it is to run, and the charge for the ad.

Therefore the classifieds are your only hope. Still, you can do a lot with the classifieds. Apart from the standard tricks such as putting his house up for sale, you can put him up as a "collector", paying cash for odd items, such as:

BOTTLE CAP COLLECTOR
Collecting beer and soda pop bottle caps, all brands. Will pay $1 for each bottle cap. Bring to 69 Easy St. Anytown, U.S.A.

You can phone in an obituary in his name, then clip it out and send it to him. While you're doing that, you can phone his friends (some of the names you have gotten from his resume, if you ran the employment ad) telling them to come to a wake at his home a certain date and referring them to the obituary in the paper.

Your local department store has a selection of mass cards and sympathy cards which you can use to add to your target's distress.

If you want to get gross you could always run a sexually-oriented ad in some of the smut papers but be prepared to pay. These publications usually do require their advertisers to pay in advance, as their advertisers are pretty scuzzy people. The ads are more expensive than those in an establishment paper and if you are paying the bill this might be important to you. In a smut paper anything goes—the sky's the limit. The only problem is that the response might be limited too. You could probably get as much response by writing his number on the toilet wall in a bar, gay or otherwise.

If you don't mind spending a few bills buy your target a subscription to one of the sleazier sex rags, preferably one catering to a perversion rather than normal sex. Make a deliberate mistake of one digit in the address, so that it goes to his neighbor's house instead of his, or the apartment next door, if that is the case. When his neighbor finds a copy of a whips and leather weekly or a homo newspaper in his mailbox it will not enhance your target's reputation. If you have a little more money to spare have a subscription sent to him at work.

Buy Now, Pay Later

Almost everyone has a credit card or two in his wallet: in fact, some people thrive on them, never paying cash but presenting a piece of plastic for everything that they buy. These cards are a great convenience but, like the telephone and other artifacts of our Twentieth Century society, they can be used to cause someone a lot of trouble.

There are several possibilities:

As pointed out earlier, if your target misplaces his wallet and you find it, you can have a lot of fun with his credit cards. However, if you take his wallet he will soon miss it, and then the fun will come to an end, for he'll report the loss of his precious cards and that will be that. If you want a somewhat longer time alone with his cards, take them out of his wallet and leave the wallet. When he finds it again the first thing he'll check is that the money is still there. If it is he might stop at that point and not discover the loss of his cards for several days or weeks, depending on how often he uses them. This allows you quite some time to make the rounds, make purchases in his name, and have them shipped to his address.

If you decide to do that be aware of what the limit is in your area. Banks and credit card companies have a limit which the merchants can accept without phoning in and getting authorization for the credit. It is usually under a hundred dollars, but is sure to climb higher as inflation feeds on the economy. The phone call for authorization can be the big stumbling block for you. If your target has discovered the loss and has reported it, the merchant will find out when he calls in, and you may find a policeman at your elbow before you can say "Bankamericard". If you keep the dollar amount of each purchase lower than the limit then the card will be accepted until its number appears on the next "hot list". Even then, how many merchants stop to check each card, anyhow?

The best way to do this is not to take his cards at all. Copy down the numbers and put them back. All you need are the numbers and expiration dates on each card you plan to use. For this purpose you don't even need the cards. He might discard an old credit purchase slip in a convenient wastebasket, from which you can later retrieve it. You can then go to work.

Many, many things can be ordered by mail and paid for with a credit card number. You don't have to send the card. Just fill in the number in the appropriate line on the coupon, sign it, and it's yours. You can have a truckload of unwanted goods on its way to him before anyone knows there's anything wrong.

If you don't want to leave even your handwriting as a trace, there are many phone-order houses that will accept your credit-card number over the phone. You can order from them and remain completely detached from the proceedings.

Yet another variant is to give his real name and address but a wrong credit-card number. Order goods that he plausibly will use, such as accessories that will fit the car he actually owns. That will not look like a joke: it will look like fraud and he will be the prime suspect.

The longer the interval between his receipt of the goods and his refusal, the more likely he will have to pay for them anyway. If you order a stereo for him and he refuses to accept it when it is delivered, he will only have the hassle of explaining things to the company that sent it to him. If, however, you arrange to have it delivered when he is out of town on a trip, and if a neighbor accepts it for him, then it is more difficult for him.

The best way to cause him a serious problem is to have it sent to a friend or acquaintance of his, ostensibly as a present. Christmastime is the best season for this, naturally, as people will gladly accept and eagerly open anything that comes to their doors. If you can arrange to have a card sent along with it, so much the better. If not, send the card separately so that it arrives a day or two before the merchandise does. If you do this when your target is out of town or when his phone has been disconnected so that the recipient of the "gift" cannot get hold of him to thank him, so much the better. By the time he finds out, the goods will have been unpacked, used, perhaps soiled or damaged, and completely unreturnable. As a complication, taking back a "present" is an awkward thing to do.

Use your imagination. With "plastic", the sky is the limit.

Guilty Secrets

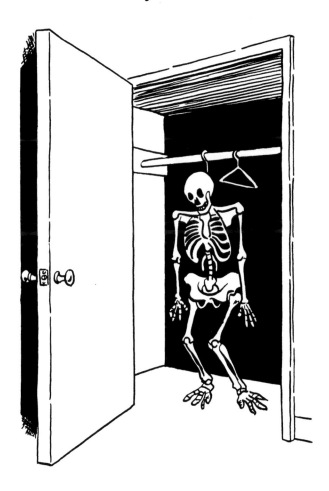

Most people have a skeleton or two in their closets, something in their past about which they have been conditioned to feel guilty. It may be something straightforward and simple, such as a prison record. It may be a family affair, such as an uncle who went insane, or an ethnic background covered up by an Anglicized name. It could be an ongoing thing, such as being a "closet" homosexual. Whatever it is, it can be a time bomb waiting to explode in your target's face. Sometimes, with a bit of luck, you can make it happen.

If you happen to find out about a guilty secret that concerns your target, you can exploit the information in several ways. For example, if your target has an ethnic background he is trying to cover up, you can send away for his birth certificate and send copies to the important people in his life (employer, club members, neighbors) with a covering letter (The man you know as "Jack Winston" had a different name when he was born—"Jacob Weinstein".) It is not as easy as it was to get a copy of a birth certificate nowadays, as the authorities have become aware of the traffic in false documentation known as "paper tripping" and have tightened their procedures. Other paperwork will do for your purpose and is easier to dig out legally.

A newspaper announcement of his birth will serve your purpose. A school yearbook page is even better, as it usually has a photo of the student and that makes it difficult for the target to deny that the person listed is really him.

A criminal record is more difficult to document from official sources but again the newspapers will often be even better for your purposes. The article might well have a photo of the target and will usually list the original charge on which he was arrested. A "rap sheet", or "yellow sheet" will list the conviction, which often is merely a guilty plea to a lesser offense. The newspaper article will be more pejorative.

The one drawback to all of this is that the available documentation may well be in another part of the country and that means that you will have to go get it, with all the attendant expenses involved. It is not always possible to do this by mail.

Sometimes you can save time and money by using the telephone. You don't have to be a detective to do a background check on your target, and doing it by phone will bring you lesser results than doing it by search warrant and subpoena, but it involves no risk to you. It is easy to phone present and former employers and find out important details about your target, such as verifying his social security number, former address and employment, date and place of birth, etc. Then you can dig back further to schools, asking for yearbooks and other records if they are available.

If you cannot do a quality job on your target you are not stalled. You can always write poison pen letters to his contacts on the assumption that some people will believe them. If your facts are correct, they may be believed even without documentation. An employer may ask him about his alleged prison record and his behavior may confirm his guilt.

If all else fails, you can resort to a total fabrication. This can be frighteningly effective. For example, if your target is a schoolteacher, a search through old newspapers will surely uncover an article about someone arrested for homosexual acts. From a current issue of the paper, you may find a photograph of your subject in connection with an award, or a school picnic, etc. A quick paste-up job and some copies run off on a photocopying machine will produce very convincing "evidence" that can be sent to his principal, members of the school board, and to parents of children attending that school. It may not result in your target's getting fired, but he will have a few uncomfortable moments because of it.

You can, if you choose, try the "blackmail" variation. A letter to your target threatening to expose his secret unless he pays up can cause him a lot of heartache. If you choose to do this, be very careful about two critical points:

1) Don't bluff. A letter that says: "I know all about you and will tell all unless you pay" will not be taken very seriously. You have to mention specific facts to show your target you know what you are talking about.

2) Don't try to actually collect money. The weakest point in any blackmail or ranson operation is collecting the money and you can be sure that the police, if your target has called them, have some sophisticated ways of tracing you if you actually pick up the money. That does not mean that you can't tell him to deliver a package of money to some invonvenient location, as long as you are not there.

As long as you do not succumb to the temptation to make some money on it, a fake blackmail scheme can do a lot for your cause. Apart from not wanting the target to know who you are, you have to face the possibility that a desperate blackmail victim may try to kill or maim his tormentor.

One way to make this work for you is to sign the name of another person. If you have another target with whom you want to get even, the choice is simple. If that is the case, you can stir the pot by having an accomplice who is totally unacquainted with either one phone each one to get things moving. Your blackmail note can say that you'll phone the target at a certain time. Your accomplice calls, tells him that he is the second target, and orders him to bring the money to his address. Then he phones the second target, identifies himself as the first one, insults him, threatens him, and tells him that he is coming right over to do him in. You will read about the results in the morning paper if it goes down too late to make the late-night news on the tube.

The Dragon's Paperwork Tail

There are a lot of official government forms that are there to be filled out to keep our bureaucracy running smoothly. Each one has its function, like a little pushbutton that starts a large machine going. If you know which button to press, you can do a lot. Specifically you can make the government your unwitting partner in harassment.

The simplest way is to start at your local post office. While you're filling out a change of address form for your target, as suggested in Volume 1 of Harassment, pick up an Alien Registration Card, too. This is a document that every alien must fill out yearly and drop into a mailbox, to be forwarded to the Immigration and Naturalization Service. Fill it out in your target's name and sooner or later he will get a letter, phone call, or a visit from the Immigration men to ask him why he had not registered in previous years, when did he enter the country, etc. There is no chance of getting him deported if he is a bona fide U.S. citizen, but if, just if, your target is an illegal alien . . .

Every January you will find Income Tax forms out for the taking in post offices, banks, and government offices. You can use these well for your purposes. You can fill out a Form 1040 in your target's name, showing him as getting a large income but without any tax payment. That will bring the "revenooers" to his door.

A more subtle way to do it is to send him a spurious W-2 form. You can only do this if you know where he works and approximately how much he earns. Send him a form showing him as having earned less than he actually did. If he does not recognize it as fake, he will send it in with his Form 1040 and eventually the government will catch up to the fact that he owes them money. The possible pitfalls in this sort of plan are that the company for which he works may have its own printed W-2s, or may have already sent them out when you send yours. Again, he might know exactly how much he earned last year and might spot the discrepancy.

In that case, another tactic might work. Fill out a fake Form 1040, attach a fake W-2, and send it in in his name. Again, do not send any payment with it and make sure that it shows that he owes money.

If you want to get really nasty send in a form that shows that the government owes him money. With a bit of luck this will go through their pipeline and he will get a check from the U.S. Treasury. That won't help him one bit, because the money's not his, and as soon as the government finds out about the error they will land on him with both feet and he will have to scurry to avoid a tax evasion and fraud charge.

There are several variants possible. If you send in a fake 1040 showing that he owes them money, you can later send in a very nasty and threatening letter in his name, telling the government people that if they don't stop dunning him for the money he will do something drastic, such as blowing up the IRS office, or shooting the revenue officer.

Perhaps the fastest way to get the government on his back is to send an obscene and threatening letter to the President of the United States. The letter will be more effective if you write it as a specific threat, mentioning a specific day when you will do him harm; say the day the President visits your city to open a new national monument, etc. It will also help if your target happens to be (luck again) a member of a fringe political group. The Secret Service will be coming around to take a close look at him very quickly.

Something similar can be done in conjunction with another tactic, that of cutting off his utilities. You can write, after the event, letters to the utility companies and to the President, Governor, and Mayor, holding them personally responsible that such a thing could happen to him and that you (he) will do them bodily harm in reprisal. That will start the avalanche.

Come Into My Hearse

You might decide, if you want to give your plan of attack a macabre twist, to phone an undertaker and have him send a hearse to your target's house to pick up his body. If you do this after placing an obituary notice in the paper and sending out mass cards, the effect will be more devastating, especially if your target is the old-fashioned sort who believes that it is sacrilegious to joke about death.

Probably every year people call up undertakers to pull a hoax of this sort. It is quite likely that you will not be believed when you make the call, unless you can be quite convincing.

We have done this exactly twice. The first time, I placed the call and was disbelieved. The second time, my wife Tina did it and pretended to be the tearful widow of the "deceased". This time it worked, and the hearse rolled up in front of the target's house at two o'clock in the morning. This sort of thing always should be done at night—it almost guarantees that the target will be at home and assures that he will be awakened. The two men went up to the target's front door, one of them carrying a body bag, a black plastic affair with a stout zipper. The target answered the door in pajamas and bathrobe, undoubtedly startled to find that these men had come to take him away, hah-hah!

Chicken, Anyone?

A chicken can be very useful. All of us have had chicken to eat. Some of us have even seen a live one from time to time. A dead one, even when bought in a supermarket, starts to smell positively awful after a couple of days without refrigeration. Chickens are so commonly available, and the price is so low, that they are very useful in a program of harassment. Let's look at some of the possibilities:

If you can risk a personal appearance, put a chicken from the supermarket, plastic and all, under the front seat of your target's car. It will take only a couple of days to get ripe, unless you are having an unusually cold winter.

If you are moving out of rented premises and you have a grudge against the landlord, a chicken or pieces thereof placed in various nooks and crannies will cause him no end of trouble when he tries to rent it again. In this case, do not put a whole chicken in one place, no matter how well concealed you think it is. The smell will lead him to it and he will find it and clean it out. Instead, get a cut-up fryer and put a wing here and a thigh there. Some possible places to put these smelly little time bombs are:

1) In the toilet tank.
2) Behind particularly heavy furniture.
3) In the stove.
4) In the wall. Unscrew a light switch and drop it in.
5) Inside furniture. Under seat cushions, in the guts of a recliner, wedged in the springs of a chair, etc.

The effect will be enhanced if the material can lay undisturbed for a few days, so that the putrefaction can set in and the juices from the rotting meat can ooze into the carpeting, furniture fabric, and any wood or other porous materials around. A good way to ensure this is to move out several days early, not telling the landlord that you've gone.

A chicken can be used to harass people other than landlords. If your target is a car dealer who sold you a lemon, a piece of chicken can be put in several of his cars, either on the showroon floor or on the lot. If you can do this just before a long weekend, so much the better. Whatever the case, after you've seeded each car with a piece of chicken, roll up the windows tightly.

If your foe is a business, so much the better. Most businesses are public or semi-public places anyway. People can go in and out without being questioned, unlike a private house. That gives you several opportunities to do damage. Chicken pieces thrown into the heater or air conditioner intake will gross out the whole place. If the intake is not accessible, placing it inside the nearest available outlet will do. All you have to do is to unscrew the register and drop it in, or throw it in as far as you can.

In a supermarket, placing pieces of chicken behind stacks of canned goods will do the job, particularly if the canned goods you choose are slow-moving items that will not be disturbed for many days. You have the advantage that you don't even have to pay for the chicken. Just put a couple of packages in your cart and plant them when nobody is looking.

If your target is a super-large company, it will more likely than not have a large lobby or public reception area. Whether you are after the phone company, a public utility, or a large insurance company that did you dirty, they all have the same features in common: a large public reception area, with few if any security guards in evidence, although they may be crawling all over the rest of their facilities.

All lobbies have furniture. The old chicken-in-the-seat-cushion trick will work here. There may be some alcoves or corridors where you can conceal your packages even better. If all else fails, visit the restroom before leaving the plant. Most of the newer ones do not smell like toilets at all, but rather clean and perfumey. You can do something about that.

At this point you might well be asking: "Why should I pay for chicken to stink up the place? Why not get a bag of feces, either my own or dog droppings, and save a little money?" Why not, indeed?

The problem is in the carrying. Your purpose is to stink up your target, not yourself, and if you walk around with a plastic bag of dog droppings in your pocket you might appear a bit conspicuous. People would begin to notice you, and, for various reasons that is what you want to avoid.

A chicken is like a time bomb—it hardly smells at all when you buy it, but in a couple of days . . .

A Bomb in the Mail

Actually sending someone explosives in the mail is illegal and in any event, your purpose is harassment, not murder. There are, however, other ways to get to someone by way of the post office, and most of them are available to you.

The first step is finding your target. If he has moved recently and you don't know where he has gone, it is easy and perfectly legal to make the post office do your work for you. Simply put several sheets of blank paper (or newspaper, or whatever) in an envelope and address it to your target at his old address. Take it to your local post office and at the counter ask the clerk for a delivery receipt with a "show address where delivered" sticker on it. If your target has filed a change of address card with the post office, so that his mail will be forwarded to his new address, your envelope will be forwarded to him and the new address will come back to you on the card.

Now that you know where he can be reached by mail you can send him some more interesting mail. Exactly what it will be depends partly on luck. If you get in your mail a free sample of a new shampoo, for example, this gives you a perfect opportunity to "doctor" it and send it to him with all the sales literature intact to calm his suspicions. Removing the shampoo from the container and substituting glue or a depilatory will cause him some problems. A squirt of hair remover will cause him a lot of grief, unless he is bald already or you think some other member of his family might use it, in which case forget the idea.

You can strike at him through his car. Other harassment books have suggested putting harmful additives in his gasoline or oil. Don't go near his car. You might be seen and recognized. Let him do the work for you, anyway. Buy a bottle of oil additive and put some grinding compound in with it, then mail it to him as a free sample. He'll put it in himself.

Some additives that can be put in with or substituted for engine oil are abrasives, epoxy resins, and sugar or corn syrup. They will all do some nasty things to his car, and cost him some money to fix, but they will not endanger life or limb as cutting the brake lines would.

A sample package of laundry detergent with some fabric dye mixed in will cause him some consternation. How would you feel if all your underwear, shirts, handkerchiefs, and bedsheets came out of the washing machine the same shade of brown?

Anything edible can be "doctored" with laxative and sent to him as a free sample, unless you are concerned that a member of his family or some other innocent person might eat it.

It you are lucky enough to work in a print shop, or have a close friend who does, you can do all sorts of wonderful things. People tend to believe things that are on paper much more readily than things that they hear. A phone call telling him that he and his wife have just won dinner for two at an expensive restaurant might arouse suspicion, but a couple of "tickets" or "coupons" arriving in the mail will usually be accepted at face value.

Knowledge of your target's tastes will be very helpful here, underlining the need for accurate information. If your target is interested in ballet, some fake tickets for the ballet will cause him some inconvenience. Don't worry about the possibility of his having bought real tickets at some time in the past and recognizing your efforts as fake. Make the "tickets" deliberately unlike the regular ones and have a legend on them such as "SPECIAL PROMO", or "CHARITY NIGHT" so that he will not be mentally comparing them with the real thing.

To twist the knife further, you can send him "gift certificates" in the name of a friend or associate who, hopefully, is as obnoxious and deserving of harassment as your target is. If you choose to do this, pick someone who is out of town or otherwise temporarily unavailable, to avoid your target phoning him up to thank him and thereby discovering the fake. You would prefer that your target plan for an evening out, hire a baby-sitter, dress up, and actually go to the event before he discovers that he has been duped. Best of all is if he can run up a bill that he must pay for, such as at a restaurant. Sending him a "GOOD WILL CARD" will do the trick here, particularly if you have a line on it that says: "Present this card when the waiter gives you the check." If you want to add insult to injury, another line of type that says: "Tip included" will do it.

Impersonation

Although covered in other chapters, impersonation is a useful tool of harassment by itself. There are several ways in which, without any additional techniques, you can cause your target much more trouble than he can handle.

Apart from the usual tactics of phoning liquor stores, pizza shops, etc. and having things sent to his house, there are ways in which you can cause your target more than just the major annoyances the usual impersonation stunt creates.

Each year charities have telethons. Other organizations, such as public TV stations, have fund-raising drives. It is easy to phone them and to pledge money, especially if it is not yours. A creative twist to this is to call up and pledge say, a thousand dollars in your target's name. Then you add: "I want this donation to be both in my name and that of my girlfriend, Anna." His wife's name is Jean and if she is watching . . .

A major variant of impersonation is called the "crossfire" technique. That involves setting one against the other while you slip away. One way it can work is like this:

You have it in for two targets, a fellow who cheated you out of some money and the local power company. If you can do it without risk, get into your target's yard and cut off his power. If not, phone to have his power cut off. Then make some crank calls to the power company in your target's name. You could also start by making some threatening and abusive phone calls about an alleged overcharge on his bill. The idea is to get him known to the power company as a crank.

The next step is to go to their office and plant pieces of chicken in their offices. After a few days, phone them and say to them: "I always thought that you stink but now you really do!" Don't make it too easy for them. Don't give your impersonated name. They'll recognize your voice sooner or later. If you are in a rural or semi-rural area you might be able to damage one of their overhead power lines. Then call them up and brag about it. The key is to have called enough people there and to have made enough of a pest of yourself so that your target's name will be remembered.

Still, it takes hard evidence to prosecute and your target will not suffer any physical punishment, although his nerves will be a frazzle after that. If you are more ambitious you can use the CB trick, which is wholly without risk, as there is not even a wire to be traced.

You have heard on the news or read in the paper from time to time of a hot-tempered CB hobbyist coming to blows with another CB user over words exchanged on the air. It is easy to get on the air and to provoke an argument with a likely candidate, challenge him to a fight, and to give your target's name and address. Sooner or later someone will respond. You can pick the likely prospects by monitoring the bands and listening to what is said. You will get a feel for the people on the air after a while and you'll be able to make a good choice on whom to pick an argument with.

Yet another way to cause your target trouble is by impersonating him on the phone, even though you don't know much more about him than his name and address. You can make enemies for him almost at will. For example, look in the telephone directory for people with strange or funny-sounding names. Call them up:

"Hello?"

"Is this Philbert Quackenbush?"

"Yes it is. What can I do for you?"

"Nothing really. I just wanted to talk to someone who had such a stupid name and find out if they're real."

"Well, now you have and I'm real. Is there anything else you want?"

"Yeah. I'd like to know if that was your father's name too. If he was a doctor, he must have been a real quack."

"Now look here . . ."

"Now I've got a nice normal name, John Smith, not like some jerks I know. All the people who live here on Easy Street have nice normal names."

"Look, if you don't like my name that's too bad, but it's really none of your business."

"Yes it is my business. You have a name like a fag would have. Maybe you are a fag. Are you married?"

"I am married but I don't care whether you like it or not."

"To what, a girl or a boy? A fag like you makes the neighborhood bad and if I ever see you on the street I'll kick your teeth down your throat. I don't live too far from you, you creep. Easy Street is only three blocks away so you'd better watch out."

"You'll kick my teeth down my throat, you miserable &$$%, I'll be right over. We'll see who's a fag!"

Unfortunately, that way can involve an innocent person who might be a perfectly nice guy. There are, however, others available whom you'd like to see come to grief. Let us say you read in the paper that a known child molester or wife beater was just acquitted or released from prison. Phone him up and tell him what you think if him:

"Hello?"

"Is this Max Fester, the babykiller?"

"Who is this?"

"I'm a decent citizen who thinks people like you should get thirty days in the electric chair with it set on 'simmer'. People on my block would lynch an asshole like you if they saw you."

"You crazy creep-who are you?"

"I'm Irving Niceguy, over here on Clean Street, where we don't like molesters like you. I don't know why your mother didn't strangle you when you were born. She was probably too busy sleeping around, though. If your father hadn't spent so much time in the gay bar he'd have been able to take care of you."

Of course, the possibilities are endless. You can call a recently released stick-up man and accuse him of child molesting. You can phone members of fringe political groups, the more militant the better, and give them the same treatment. You can call up a wife beater and invite him to pick on someone his own size. There is no limit to the conflicts you can instigate if you have the imagination.

Giving Him the Business

If your target owns his own business, hitting at him there can produce even more rewarding results than hitting at him "where he lives". This is just as well, as the odds are that anyone against whom you have a grievance will be someone with whom you have a business, rather than personal relationship.

You are more likely to be shafted by a stranger than by a friend or relative. At least eight hours of your day are spent at work, if you are like most Americans. Some of the rest of those hours are spent shopping or dealing with tradesmen, such as an air conditioner repairman. Few of us buy a car from a relative, yet many, many complaints involve cars. Not many of us have a friend or a relative who owns an insurance company or a supermarket.

When you are sold a car that turns out to be a lemon, when an insurance company reneges on your coverage because they are taking advantage of the fine print in a policy that is purposely written to be obscure, when you are cheated by a company with which you are dealing, you are a victim of a white-collar crime. White-collar crime is far more common than "street crime", yet it goes unpunished more often because it does not involve violence. The laws concerning white-collar crime are weak and loosely enforced. If you become the victim of a white-collar criminal, you have less chance of getting satisfaction than if you are the victim of a street crime—

—Unless you do it yourself, of course. Where the law stops, the vigilante begins, and there are times when you have to be your own vigilante. If you are right, but the law will not support you, then you have to take the law into your own hands.

Let's take a quick look at the types of business dealings which you may find victimizing you, and let's assess your chances of getting satisfaction by various methods in each case.

When you are dealing with a large corporation you are, in a way, the most helpless. If you are treated unfairly, it is often the result of a policy decided at the highest level, by executives whom you will never meet and who don't even know that you exist. If the law does not give you satisfaction it is difficult to trace the chain of responsibility to find out who is really to blame. The company's representatives with whom you deal are usually people on the lowest rungs of the corporate ladder, hired hands, and are not responsible for the company's policy. For example, when you have a problem with the phone company, taking it out on the operator is pointless. She has to obey orders if she wants to keep her job, and the phone company exercises strict discipline to see that she does her job the way its policy dictates.

Sometimes, however, an employee of a large company will exceed his orders and give you a hard time thereby. For example, an insurance salesman who is greedy for commissions and who will lie to you about the coverage of a policy that he wants you to buy from him is the type of employee who is directly responsible for any grief you may have later. There are personality problems in large companies as well as small ones, and if you run into this sort of situation you can more easily cope with it.

Complaining to higher management can often get you some sort of satisfaction. At least, you will quickly find out if the company is responsive to your needs.

Not so if you have to resort to the law. It is easy to say: "Sue the bastards." but it takes a lot of time, effort, and money to do so and many times you are stymied by the delaying tactics the defendant will use, as well as the normal delays built into the law. Collecting damages can take years. Corporations have large staffs of lawyers, professionals at dealing with people such as you, whose jobs involve insulating top management from the hassles of going to court for every complaint. You will suffer months and perhaps years of anxiety and aggravation, but the top corporate brass won't be losing any sleep over it.

Complaining to Ralph Nader may get you some results but don't count on it. If your case does not happen to tie in with something that he is working on at the moment you may have a long wait. In any event he is not a law enforcement agency and has no official powers. Calling the SEC, FDA, or another Federal regulatory agency might get you something but they are very reticent about fighting the big boys, and in any event the pace at which the Federal agencies move is slow indeed. Don't hold your breath.

Taking action on your own will get you the fastest results. You have to decide whether you will take action against the company as a whole or a specific individual in it. Once you decide that you can work from there. Often, the same methods that work against an individual will work against a

129

large corporation. Sometimes they are even more effective. Diverting the mail of a large corporation can result in larger losses than an individual could incur in a lifetime. If you are an employee or former employee, you have inside knowledge that can be invaluable in pinpointing vulnerable spots in the company's operations.

The medium-sized business is easier to deal with, if only because you are not dealing with a faceless monolith but real people down at your level. For example, if you have a problem with a car dealership you can go right to the "top" without too much trouble. It is usually possible to get in to see the boss if you are persistent and cannot get satisfaction at a lower level. It is also easier to pinpoint the responsibility for the problems that you are having. For example, if you have been sold a "lemon", you can usually dump the problem in the sales manager's lap, or the owner's, not the poor mechanic who is struggling to fix the car every time you bring it back. This makes it easier for you. It is harder to hide behind the veil of "company policy" when the man you are dealing with is the one who makes the policy.

Pinpointing the responsibility is more than half the battle and once you have done that you can make a tangible plan for action, if you cannot get satisfaction any other way. However, keep in mind that a smaller company is less able to hold you off if you decide to sue. Often, just the mention of legal action will make them sit up and take notice, so don't ignore that possibility.

Finally there is the small businessman, the tradesman with whom you deal directly. These are usually an honest bunch but they have their bad ones in their number too. The bad businessman may be your landlord, mechanic, butcher lawyer, or even doctor. Yes, doctor. A doctor is not only a healer; he is a businessman. Some would even say that a doctor is a businessman first and a healer second. In any event, many people have justifiable grievances against doctors. This is for one outstanding reason: they expect you to pay whether they do their job or not. A photographer whose picture doesn't come out does not send you a bill. A plumber who does not fix the leak usually keeps at it until he does or he tells you that your problem is more than he can handle and does not charge you. Even the most hard-boiled car dealer would not expect you to pay if he did not deliver a car to you. Doctors present their bills, whether you live or die, whether you recover or not.

When dealing with the small businessman the situation is simpler for you. There is usually a one-to-one relationship and you know where you stand. You either get satisfaction directly or you resort to other means.

If the situation goes against you and you find that you must resort to harassment to get satisfaction, you'll find that in one way it is easier to strike hard against a businessman at his place of business than at his home. The reason is that he must sit there and take it. If things get too hot for him at home he can always move out or move away. He can go to a relative's home, or to a motel, or out of town to a suburb. If he has a family his problem will be more complicated but he can do it if he has to.

A company cannot pull up stakes and disappear and remain in business. A company cannot get an unlisted phone. Moving even across the street is a major undertaking and in any event it will not stop the harassment.

Some specific techniques which will work well against a business, apart from the simple and effective ones of diverting the mail, having the telephone service stopped, and the utilities cut off, are these:

Generate a lot of wrong number calls to tie up his phone and to keep him or his employees busy answering calls. It is easy to place an innocent-sounding classified ad offering a house for sale at a very attractive price, but showing his business phone. Posters and fliers giving his phone for any reason under the sun will work. You can have him getting calls for a suicide clinic, free green stamps, alcoholic counseling, or even dial-a-prayer. Every time you go into a supermarket which has a public bulletin board, fill out a few cards and put them up. Have people call him for a baby-sitter, to have their lawns mowed, their TVs fixed, cats spayed for free, abortion counseling, etc., etc.

Posters and fliers advertising spurious free offers can have him climbing the walls. A car dealer can be besieged by people waving fliers entitling them to a free dinner for two just for taking a test drive in his new Super Perkle Eight.

Garages can be made to offer free tune-ups or oil changes but to be effective this should be for one day only, to get maximum concentration on that one day.

Doctors' offices can be crowded by people demanding the "free" first aid book he is giving away.

The power company will feel the effect if you put out fliers offering a "free" 300-page electric cooking book. Specify that the customer must come to the main office in person to pick up his "free" copy, and that coffee and cake will be available to all.

Most businesses have an "open house" every now and then. You can arrange for an extra one. "Buffet dinner and the bar stays open until midnight."

A nasty that can be done to almost any sort of business is to smuggle a gallon can of gasoline onto the premises and to put it in a convenient closet. If you don't want to be recognized have an accomplice do it. The can should be clearly marked "gasoline" and preferably should be the sort that you can buy in an auto store. Then you phone the Fire Department and ask to speak with the Fire Marshall, or Fire Safety Officer. Tell him that such-and-such a company keeps gasoline in an unsafe place, that people are constantly smoking near it, and that you are an employee and afraid of an accident. To protect yourself against reprisals you refuse to give your name but you can tell him exactly where the gasoline is stored. Then let the pot boil.

A restaurant can be sabotaged quite well by carrying in some dog droppings in a plastic bag in your pocket. Old, dried up ones will do nicely for this, so there is no need to risk carrying around a pocketful of sloppy, smelly goo. Try to get a booth rather than a table in the middle of the floor. You want a seating arrangement where people cannot easily see under the table while you shake the turds out of the plastic bag. If you can manage to do this at several tables so much the better. Then you call the board of health. In most localities it is illegal to bring animals into a restaurant, except for seeing eye dogs. You tell the board of health that you are an employee of the restaurant, that you have seen dogs other than seeing eye dogs constantly brought into the restaurant, and that the dogs are allowed to defecate on the premises. You add that you need your job, therefore you want to remain anonymous, but that the physical evidence is there to see if they send an inspector over to check it out.

In most states it is legal to buy a hypodermic syringe. Food coloring is commonly available in the spice section of the supermarket. If you want to "get" a supermarket it is very easy to buy some assorted fruit, take it home, and "doctor" it by injecting food coloring, which will not harm anyone who swallows it but it will certainly make it look queer. Red and yellow mixed together, with a touch of blue, will give you a shade of brown. A shot of this in an apple, banana, or orange will impel the person who bought it to return it. A few incidents will cause an intolerable hassle for a supermarket manager.

Getting the fruit where it will be picked up by someone else is easy—carry it in your pockets. This could be called shoplifting in reverse and it is almost foolproof. Nobody expects you to carry merchandise into a store and put it on the shelf.

Supermarkets and other types of food stores are very vulnerable to this sort of operation. There are so many people going in and out each day that it is impossible to guard against this form of harassment.

A restaurant, cocktail lounge, hotel or motel can be used as the site of a "meeting". Classified ads, posters and fliers can all be used to announce the news to the world. The organization need not be a real one, as long as the message reaches people who can be induced to attend. It will be most effective if you can get your members from the sleazier part of town, or from the less wholesome classes. An alcoholic revival meeting, with posters in many bars, will be good for some disturbance. A spurious ethnic organization can have the management climbing the walls. A "welfare union", with members from the slums, will not enhance the hotel's atmosphere.

"Free samples" can be used to great effect if your target is a machine shop, or power station; any place that has machinery that uses grease. Send them some, spiked with an abrasive that will grind away at delicate and expensive bearings.

"Help wanted" ads are a sure-fire winner whatever type of business it is. A lot can be accomplished, depending on how you word the ad. Some possible first lines are:

"Messenger, $7.00/hr. must have own motorcycle. . ."
"Homosexuals needed for research project, pays well."
"Model trainees, $10.00/hr. to start, no exp. necessary."
"Bodyguard trainees, $10.00/hr. to start, no exp."

There is a limitation, however. Most companies close up at night. You can only really go to work on them during business hours. You won't be disturbing anybody's sleep by arranging for after-midnight phone calls.

There are ways to do something, though, even on weekends. If the company has a sizeable parking lot, an ad in a biker's magazine, or an underground newspaper will bring them in if it's worded like this:

"Perkle Eight Car Dealer sponsoring picnic Sunday morning at its lot on Able Avenue. Free beer, refreshments. Party starts 8 A.M."

Alternatively, you could have the party start at 9 P.M., after they've locked up and gone home. Whatever you choose to do, make sure that there is a tub full of beer there to get things going. If your guests come and see nobody there, they might get angry and trash the place but they also might just assume they'd made a mistake and go home. Start the beer flowing to get them drunk, however, and things will start happening.

With the profusion of newspapers around, local, establishment, special interest, and ethnic, you can advertise in a number of them to get more people to come. You can have a Black Power Rally and Picnic at the same place and time. Mix a few other groups in and the results will be very interesting.

134

All of this is going to cost you some money. It is hard to estimate how much, but actually the price is cheap. If a company or businessman has done you dirty, what is satisfaction worth to you? For a comparison, have you taken a look at lawyers' fees lately? Harassment, even if you have to spend a couple of hundred dollars to do it right, is a bargain.

Free Samples

Introducing your target to various "free samples" will give you a bit of satisfaction, if those free samples are properly modified. Some of this depends on luck, as we have noted in an earlier chapter. If you get a free sample in the mail you can add something to it and send it on to your target. If you don't have any such handy, you can make your own. All you need is a rubber stamp and a typewriter.

The rubber stamp, which you can have made up for a very few dollars at any print shop or stationer, has the name and address of a fictitious company. You use it to stamp a sheet of typewriter paper and another, smaller sheet, which will serve as a label. You type your target a letter, under this improvised letterhead, which reads something like this:

Dear Mr. McNasty;

Enclosed is a sample of our new furniture polish. We are a new company with a revolutionary new invention for polishing furniture and we are sending free sample cans of it to selected people to try out. Use it for as long as you like. If you need more ask us for it when we contact you. All that we ask is that you tell us how you like it when we contact you.

To use—spray it on the furniture and let it soak in for an hour. Remove with soft cloth. For best results let it soak for longer than an hour, preferably overnight.

Sincerely,

J.P. Niceguy,
Marketing Director,
Nu-Way Corp.

The label on the spray can reads simply: "Furniture Polish Type 2599".

The contents of the can are what makes this most interesting. In reality, you have bought a can of brown spray paint and soaked off the label. If the label is silk-screened on, you can get it off by rubbing with auto rubbing compound. The instructions you send with the "polish" ensure that your target will give it time to dry.

This is something that you can do only once or twice to your target. However, you can choose from among a large variety of products to doctor.

Another way to introduce a doctored product into his home is to have a friend of yours pass out samples on the block. This is more costly but the results might well be worth it if you choose the product with care.

Yet another way is to have a friend pose as a door-to door salesman. A variation on this is to have your accomplice drive a truck and peddle bags of fertilizer at a rock-bottom price. Your target's wife might well buy one. If she does not, he can tell her that he sold so many to neighbors already and that this is his last bag, that he doesn't want to take it back with him, what the hell, she can have it for nothing. People love to get something for nothing. Of course, the fertilizer has a cupful of grass killer mixed in with it. By the time she uses it and sees the effect, your accomplice will be long gone.

Appendix A—Contaminants

The following is a short list of commonly available contaminants which, when introduced into or substituted for certain commonly used products, will cause varying amounts of destruction. The advantages of these materials is that they are available almost everywhere you go, without a prescription or a special license. Each item is listed with its suggested use and the source from which it is available. Ways of introducing it into your target's environment are found elsewhere in this book.

PEPPER EXTRACT - A colorless hot sauce that will spoil the taste of various foods. It can also be added to the glue on stamps and envelopes. It is to be found in drug stores and supermarkets under various trade names sold as products to stop nail-biting in children.

LINSEED OIL - When substituted for 3-in-1 oil it will do the oppossite of lubrication. As it oxidizes it will dry out and bind the moving parts. When applied to sewing machines, vacuum cleaners, etc. it will run up some repair bills. When introduced as a crankcase oil or gasoline additive it will clog up and damage the engine. Available in department stores, sporting goods stores, and leather shops.

MOTH BALLS - Whether made of camphor or para, these will dissolve in gasoline or hot engine oil. Much more effective in clogging up an engine than sugar, as sugar does not dissolve well in gasoline. Available anywhere.

WAX CRAYONS - When introduced into a clothes dryer, these will stain the clothing being dried. Use several different colors for maximum effect. You can get these in toy stores, stationers, and five-and-dimes.

WATER- When poured into the gas tank, this will stop a car cold. A small amount of water can be packaged as a gas additive. When poured in, it will sink to the bottom of the tank, being heavier than gasoline, and will go into the fuel line quickly. This substance is available anywhere without a prescription. In a real emergency you can substitute urine.

BATTERY ACID- When substituted for fabric cleaner, this substance will quickly rot fabric. When used as a gas or oil additive, it will cause corrosion in the engine. In gasoline, it will also stop the car. It is sold in automotive stores.

FOOD COLORING - A harmless, edible coloring that can be used to make anything edible look queer. Available in any food store.

YEAST - When added to any liquid containing sugar or sugary substances, such as corn syrup, will cause fermentation. This will result in bubbles, alcohol, and carbon dioxide being produced. The CO_2 will cause any sealed container to eventually rupture, possibly with explosive force. Two cautions—some products contain a preservative which will prevent the yeast from working, and if you introduce yeast into a glass container, the resulting explosion could injure an innocent person. Yeast can be bought in any food store. Any yeast will do: it doesn't have to be brewer's yeast.

PHENOLPHTHALEIN - A powerful laxative. This white, tasteless powder is the active ingredient in that chocolate laxative that you see in drug stores. In its pure form, it can be mixed into various food products to cause diarrhea. It is available at a chemical supply house and sometimes in children's chemistry sets.

EDIBLE ACIDS - Lemon juice, which contains citric acid, and vinegar, which has about 5% acetic acid, will strongly affect the taste of most foods. When injected into a carton of milk will make it sour and undrinkable. Fruits and vegetables are vulnerable to this treatment too.

ABRASIVES - Carborundum and sand are two commonly available abrasives that will do wonders when introduced into your target's crankcase. Use a fine grade, so that it will pass through the oil filter and recirculate in his engine. Some engines, such as that in the Volkswagen Beetle, do not have an oil filter, and this makes the effect more immediate and more profound. Don't forget that an abrasive will "improve" other products too, such as furniture polish, auto cleaning compound, car wax, floor wax, chassis grease, wheel bearing grease, and vinyl cleaner. Carborundum is sold in auto stores. Sand can be picked up off the ground, in many areas.

143

DEFOLIANTS - Grass and weed killers can be spread directly on your target's lawn or flowers, but why bother? Mix it into a bag of plant or lawn food. Available from any garden shop.

SHOE POLISH - Very nasty when introduced into a clothes dryer. Can be bought anywhere.

SPRAY PAINT - Relabel it as insecticide, for best results. Be sure to pick a nice color. Bought in supermarkets, paint stores, etc. Can also be relabeled as air freshener, mothproofing, or furniture polish. It will also do well as a substitute for glass cleaner or fabric protector.

Appendix B—Basic Tactics of Disruption

This is a guide to the basic thinking about disrupting your target's lifestyle, which is the fundamental mechanism of harassment. Here is the framework within which you can examine every aspect of your target's lifestyle and determine what you can do to him in the easiest way and with the least risk to yourself.

No book can tell you in detail exactly what to do to any target at all. It is possible to put forth a few basic guidelines, and to list some tactics which can be adapted to a wide range of situations, but it is not possible to write out a plan that will be equally useful in all cases. Each target has to be examined in detail, the vulnerable points studied, and the best way of attacking them planned out. You have to be the architect of your campaign against your target, and it is your brainpower that will prevail.

List, on a sheet of paper if you must, everything that your target is or does. Where he lives, the car he drives, what he does for a living, his telephone number, etc., are all important. When you have a heading for each item, then examine each one to determine the best way for you to attack it. You will find that your target is more vulnerable in some areas than in others. You will also find that some methods of attack are easier for you than some others. From these factors you will make your plan.

The methods of attack are:

1) Destruction. Physical destruction is the most obvious, and yet the least suitable method in many cases. You can burn down his house, but that is a felony, you may kill innocent people, you have to be physically present on the scene, and probably the situation doesn't justify such extreme measures, anyway.

Destruction can work, though, in certain minor ways. If, for example, he leaves his bankbook or driver's license where it is accessible to you without his knowledge, then destroying them can cause your target some hardship in getting them replaced.

2) Disruption. Often, it is possible to get the same results without physical damage. For example, you could physically cut his telephone wire, or you could make a spurious phone call to the telephone company and have his phone temporarily disconnected, with much less risk to yourself.

3) Diversion. This works very well on his mail. You need not set fire to his mailbox to deprive him of his mail, nor do you need to hold up the mailman. Filing a change of address

card with the post office will do it perfectly. You can compound his difficulties by sending a change of address notice to all of the magazines to which he subscribes, book clubs, etc.

4) Interdiction. Sometimes, a temporary interruption will do a lot more harm than is apparent at first. For example, if your target's company uses computers, a temporary power outage will cause them to lose their memories, which can cause a lot of hassle. Also, many industrial processes will be sensitive to a power outage. Cement can set right in the mixer, chemicals will go stale right in the vat, if even a few hours' interdiction of the power supply can be arranged.

The supply of water is often sensitive too. It is as easily interdicted.

5) Saturation. This is the opposite of diversion. You cause your target to have more traffic than he can handle. Saturation works by having a lot of mail or phone calls hitting him at the same time, keeping him and/or his staff occupied telling the callers that they have the wrong number, or sending back unordered goods, etc.

6) Invasion. This means that you have traffic hitting him at odd hours, when he least expects it, or people coming to his home or place of business for spurious reasons, overcrowding the facilties. It is easy to arrange for him to get phone calls in the early hours of the morning, disturbing his sleep. Causing people to come to the parking lot of a company for a "picnic" is another example of invasion.

7) Commitment. Getting people to expect and demand things from your target which he either cannot supply or did not promise, or both, is commitment. "Free" offers are one way to use commitment. Ordering merchandise in his name is another, as the vendor will expect payment.

8) Isolation. Sending clients a notice that a company is going out of business, or moving to another address, is a way of cutting off traffic and isolating it. Companies that depend a lot on daily client contact are particularly vulnerable to this tactic. A variation on this theme is to send the employees a telegram that the company will be closed the next day, and not to report for work.

There is a lot of overlapping between categories here, and the same action can fall under several different headings. Does calling up a restaurant's towel service and having the linens delivered to another address constitute disruption, diversion, or interruption? It is pointless to argue about it. The different categories merely are a framework for thinking about the problem and a way to stimulate you to think about it in different ways, and to see it from several different sides. The more flexible you can be in your thinking, the better the ways that you will devise to harass your target.

It is also important to avoid thinking that these tactics work only against physical objects. If you can fabricate "evidence" that shows your target to be an ex-con, or a child molester, you are destroying his reputation, something which is intangible but no less real than his house or his car.

Other Sources of Ideas

The *Harassment* book by George Carpenter, although now out of print, is a book of more forceful measures, on the order of trashing your target's house and the like.

Another book along the same lines is *Get Even*, by George Hayduke, and is published by Paladin Press. This is a collection of odds and ends arranged in alphabetical order. A valuable part of this book which you should not overlook is the bibliography at the end, which lists many books dealing directly or tangentially with the subject of harassment. The fact that he erroneusly lists me as having written Carpenter's book does not diminish the value of the list. I have read many of the books on it and can confirm that they are worthwhile reading if you have the patience to go through them.

Be warned, however, that some of the ideas that you will find in other books are downright illegal, as are some of the ideas presented here, but more seriously can result in harm to innocent persons. Moreover, some of them involve action so direct, such as poisoning or arson, that you take a great risk of getting caught and prosecuted. That means the slammer.

Odds and Ends

800 NUMBERS - These are special toll-free numbers assigned to various companies which do a lot of telephone business. Often, you will see advertisements for magazines, book clubs, and other sorts of merchandise listing an 800-number that you can call to place your order. This enables you to phone in orders in your target's name without getting involved in

any paperwork. Some companies ask that you pay by credit card, and it helps to find out your target's credit card number, as explained in another chapter in this volume. Often, however, the company will send the merchandise and bill your target by mail, enabling you to operate by knowing just his name and address.

PHENOLPHTHALEIN - The correct pronunciation is: FEE-NUL-FTHA-LEEN; accents on the first and third syllables.

CREDIT CHECK - If you are a small businessman yourself you may be a member of a credit reporting bureau. If you are, you can find out a lot about your target by having a credit check run on him. If not, you might still be able to find out by impersonating your target and asking to see your file, which they are required by law to show you. Proper preparation involves phoning them first, ostensibly to find out if they have a file on you before you make the trip. If they do, ask what, if any, I.D. you have to show to be allowed to see your file.

SOCIETY COLUMN - If you can obtain a head and shoulders photograph (sometimes known as a "mug shot") of your target, it will make this one more effective. An announcement that he or she is to be married can cause him or her some embarrassment, particularly if he or she is already married or engaged to someone else. The pain will be particularly acute if your target is having an extra-marital affair and you name the co-respondent as the other party to the engagement.

FOOD SPOILAGE - If you have a grievance against a restaurant, food wholesaler, meat packing plant or butcher, any sort of business that keeps a large quantity of refrigerated or frozen food on the premises, find out if and when they close for vacation before you do ANYTHING to them. If they do, that is the time to strike, and the blow will be so devastating that it will be worth waiting for. Arrange for the electric power to be cut off at that time. All of that food in cold storage will spoil. A short power outage will not work, because the great mass of that cold food takes a long time to warm up, but a week or two without power guarantees the results.

Of course, after you've caused their food to spoil feel free to do other things that you had refrained from doing earlier to avoid putting them on their guard.

THE SECRET SIGN - The Greek letter Lambda, which looks like an upside-down "y", has recently come to signify to those in the know that the establishment displaying it on its sign or in its advertisements caters to gays or is owned by gays. This is, in effect, a secret recognition signal that homosexuals have between themselves. You may be able to cause your target some difficulty or embarrassment by taking advantage of this.

If your target is a business running a display ad in a magazine or a newspaper you may be able to have this symbol inserted in the ad. If you happen to know about the ad before it runs, or if it runs on a regular basis, a typewritten note to the advertising department, enclosing a sample of the letter and a rough layout of the ad showing where you want it placed, should do the trick. The letter can be found in the appendix of many dictionaries, as many of them list the Greek alphabet. If the ad runs regularly, this stunt should be a snap.

This symbol is used mainly for bars, health clubs, and spas, but why not be a bit creative? After all, a gay bakery or a gay plumber is not totally out of the question.

It might even be possible to paint the letter on the sign displayed in front of the business. You can do this on a weekend, when it is closed, as a rule. The police will not stop to investigate someone painting on a sign, as long as it does not look like vandalism, with large smears of paint. Another possibility is to phone a sign painter if you are reluctant to approach the premises yourself.

THE OLD PHONE CALL FROM THE EX TRICK - If your target is married a trick that will probably cause him a lot of grief or at least a lot of explaining is to have someone of the same sex telephone his wife at home when he is not there. The dialogue might go something like this:

Friend: "Hello, can I speak to Johnny?"
Wife: "Johnny's not here. Can I take a message or have him call you?"
F: "Oh, no, that's all right. I just wanted to find out how he was getting along."
W: "Who is this?"
F: "Oh, I'm sorry, I'm Mary, his ex-wife. Are you the one he's married to now?"

Does the main idea start to become clear? In this case there is no attempt to be furtive or to generate suspicion by seeming to have something to hide. It's all out in the open. Let us proceed with the imaginary dialogue as the plot sickens:

W: "I didn't know he was married before!"
F: "Oh, yes, didn't Johnny tell you? Oh, well, I guess he wouldn't have. He was always so quiet about everything, even with me. He never told me that there had been another wife before me, either, and I didn't find out until I accidentally found the divorce papers in his stuff one day while I was cleaning."

Let's take a break again and have a close look at what's just happened. Many people have been married before, and someone claiming to be the ex- will usually be accepted at face value, unless the wife knows the ex- personally. Even if the target has not been married before, this should be no problem. "Didn't he tell you?" is the answer to everything, putting the burden on the wife. Another feature is the explanation about finding divorce papers by "accident". This will plant the suggestion in the wife's head that perhaps she could find out a couple of things by looking through her husband's possessions. This also might stop her from telling him about the phone call until she had had the opportunity to check things out by going through his stuff, thereby denying him the opportunity to make a convincing denial.

154

Now, many men have things that are hard to explain away, even in the normal course of events. The wife's search might turn up, among other things:

An unexplained motel receipt.
A package of prophylactics. She uses the pill.
A compromising letter or two.
A bankbook she didn't know about.

Let's go on with the dialogue:

W: "When were you married to him?"

F: "A couple of years before you met him, I guess. I heard about it through friends after we broke up. I hope you two are happy together. Do you plan to have any children? I know he was down on kids but I didn't expect him to force me to have that abortion."

W: "Abortion? No, I didn't know, I mean no, he never did say he didn't want kids."

F: "Well, that must be because you're white. He always said he didn't want a kid that was half-and-half, and he didn't like my family, either."

W: "No, I didn't know all this. How long were you married?"

A pause here. We see that the poison needle has been slipped in, with that business about the abortion and the race problem. Now it is time to authenticate the caller. The wife may well suspect that this is a practical joke or a malicious prank, but the doubts can be erased by telling her things that only a wife or lover would be likely to know, but which could be found out by other means. A mole on the buttocks can be seen in a locker room as well as in bed, but if the effort sounds convincing then it will do the trick. Here's another way to do it that covers all the bases, even if you have never seen your target in person:

F: "We were married a couple of years. Hey, tell me, did Johnny ever get circumcised? He said he was going to get it done when we split up."

155

Again, this puts the burden on the wife. Whatever she says, she can only conclude that the caller KNOWS. Another possibility is to use any special knowledge you may have, such as neighborhood gossip. Let us say the target really was married before, and that his real ex- was very friendly with your wife or girlfriend, and that they talked, and that your wife told you some intimate details that she had heard about your target. We go on with the dialogue:

W: "I don't want to talk about that. Anyway, it isn't really any of your business anymore. You're not married to him."

F: "I'm sorry, you're right, of course. You sound very bitter. I guess the time we spent at the marriage counselor didn't do him any good. I don't know what the gal he was messing around with ever saw in him. Maybe she just did it because they both worked at XYZ Advertising and she thought she could get a promotion through him."

We pause again. If the target actually does or did work at XYZ, and if there really was or is some hanky-panky going on, the effect will be somewhat like that of a hand grenade going off in a broom closet. Let's listen in a bit more:

W: "I know Johnny doesn't play around on me. I can tell."

F: "Well, maybe he's changed, learned something from the last time. Does he still keep those homo magazines around? I never thought he was queer but that did seem funny."

See how it can go? The possibilities are endless and only the sky is the limit.

DIRTY CREDIT TACTICS - A federal law passed in 1978 makes it illegal for a collection agency to telephone a debtor at work or to browbeat him in an unethical manner. This law covers phoning him at home in the middle of the night, telling his neighbors or his boss that he owes money, or posing as a lawyer or police officer in an effort to collect the debt. Any collection agency that tries such tactics today will be in serious trouble.

Of course, if you are harassing someone, you can ignore that law — it doesn't apply to you, or at least enforcing it will be impossible. It is easy to get a trustworthy confederate whose voice is not known to the target or to any other people you choose to involve to call up and pose as a collection agency. Many people do not even know that some collection tactics are illegal, and if your target is one of these he will just sit there and take it. He may try to convince his boss and his neighbors that he does not really owe any such money but it will do him more harm than good to try, as it puts him strictly on the defensive. If he tries to report the tactics to the authorities it will still do him no good, as he will not give them anything solid to go on.

If you use a fictitious collection agency name he will find that the object of his complaint has vanished into thin air. If you use a real one it will cause the people at the agency some effort in denying that he is one of their "accounts" and it will waste their time, the target's time, and the time of the regulatory agency in checking the complaint out. It won't bounce back on you.

Let's look at how a phone call to his boss might turn out:

Confederate: "Hello, this is Mr. Nichols of the Acme Credit Collection Agency. I'd like to know Mr. Target's weekly salary."

Boss: "We don't give out that information over the phone. Why do you need to know, anyway?"

Confederate: "It will help your employee if you co-operate, Mr. Boss. He owes a lot of money on that new car of his and he seems to have gotten in way over his head as far as the money he owes on it."

At this point let's note that it always helps to have a dash of truth to embellish the fiction. If the target really has bought a new car recently and drives it to work, then that will be a convenient peg upon which to hang the rest of the story. If he has just had a vacation in Bermuda, that's another possibility. It pays to know something about what your target has been doing.

Confederate: "We'd also like to know if you can persuade Mr. Target to pay voluntarily. If he co-operates we won't have to slap a garnishment on his salary. That will help you, too. I'm sure you wouldn't want to have one of our collection agents coming to your office every Friday afternoon to pick up the check."

That isn't how collection agencies really work and if the employee's paycheck is garnisheed by the court the agency does not send an agent around every payday to physically pick up the check from the employee. That would be too expensive in manpower. The target's boss, however, may not know this. He may never have had an employee's pay garnisheed, in which case you can tell him anything within reason and he will probably believe it. Note that it is important to present an attitude of helpfulness to the boss. Show that you are trying to help everyone solve the problem with the least trouble and you will score the best effort. If you try to get nasty and threatening with the boss, you will probably get the boss solidly on your target's side, generating sympathy for him. Ask for co-operation, but don't threaten.

Boss: "I'm sorry, but we have a policy that we don't discuss our employees' wages on the phone. If you'll send us a letter, a request on your letterhead, we'll see what we can do."

Many companies take this attitude. After all, anyone can claim to be anybody over the phone. Don't be put off by this type of answer. Your main object is not to find out what your target earns; in fact, you probably already know if you've done your homework. Your purpose in calling is to make the boss think his employee is in big trouble and that some of it will rub off on him. Let's go on:

Confederate: "We'll be glad to send you a letter or even pay you a personal visit, if that will help, but we are trying to settle this matter informally. If you can persuade him to pay what he owes voluntarily it will save everybody concerned a lot of hassle. What percentage of his pay do you think he can hand over every week?"

Note the finesse of technique here: Always try to end with a question. That way, you may forestall the boss asking you a question you can't answer.

Boss: "I don't know. I'd have to ask him."

Persistent and polite effort pays off. Now you've got the beginning of co-operation. Be wary of what could turn into a trap, though.

Boss: "When I find out, where should I call you to tell you?"

Ignore the question. Come back with your own statement and question.

Confederate: "We're going to be calling him at home tonight to find out how he plans to pay us and a few other details. Right now we're going to call up his bank and it would help if you could talk to him this afternoon if your busy schedule allows it. Do you think you could find the time to do that?"

A good comeback. Again, you end with a question. That way you keep the situation under control. You might want to go a step further, though. Here's one way to do it:

Confederate: "We'd like to try every reasonable step to settle this before going to court. We'd like to sit down with you and Mr. Target and talk over ways and means of paying this account. My manager, Mr. Gentry, and I would like to come over there at a time that is convenient to you both and meet with you both. We know that your business day is a very crowded one but perhaps we could meet you at your office after business hours?"

159

Note the barb concealed behind the cloak of politeness and consideration. You do not propose to barge in on him during business hours but, having consideration for his busy schedule (and incidentally for his importance as a business-man) you offer to come after normal hours. If he accepts, you have gotten him to agree to stay at work late. He will also have kept the target with him, inconveniencing them both.

Now let us say that the appointment is for six o'clock the next afternoon. Naturally, you and "Mr. Gentry" don't show up. Don't, however, just vanish from sight. You can twist the knife by phoning the boss at a quarter after six and explaining to him that you and Mr. Gentry have been tied up in a meeting and will be a little late and would appreciate it if they could wait for you. Tell him that you will be leaving in a few minutes and that you will be there within half an hour.

Half an hour later you phone again and tell the now surely exasperated boss that a long-distance call came in for Mr. Gentry and that you were thereby further delayed. Tell him that you are leaving right now and to make it up to him for the inconvenience of the long wait you and Mr. Gentry would like to take them to dinner at a restaurant in the area. Tell him that you will meet them there.

If you think that this is too much, that they will not believe all of this malarkey, consider that if the boss has swallowed the story of the alleged debt so far, he is a credu-lous fellow and will believe it. Just as a last effort, though, call up the restaurant after the time you estimate that they should have arrived and ask to speak to the boss (Mr. Target's boss, that is). Explain to him that Mr. Gentry had to stop at home to pick up some money to pay for the meal and that you should be there within a few minutes. Tell him to order and start without you. Play it right to the end.